Revealing Secrets to Streamlining Technology

What Every Business Owner Must Know to Compete

Kevin Fream, MCITP
kfream@matrixforce.com
(918) 622-1167
matrixforce.com
kevinfream.com
linkedin.com/in/kevinfream

Published by Matrixforce, Tulsa, Oklahoma
www.matrixforce.com

First Edition
ISBN No:
978-0692921746

Printed in the United States of America

10 9 8 7 6 5 4 3 2 1

Dedication

Eclipse the competition by streamlining technology.

To the financial and professional service business owners who grow companies – and their families and staff that support them. You are the driving force of our economy and inspired source of our freedom.

Table of Contents

Introduction

This book is for bankers, doctors, lawyers, accountants, engineers, and other related professionals that struggle with Information Technology (IT) support. 80% of my business is in Oklahoma and surrounding states, but financial and professional service owners across the nation can capitalize on these secrets to streamlining technology.

The most important thing I can tell you is that the business logic and premises you operate on for technology are dated by at least 15 - 20 years. If we were in the middle of the industrial revolution, that wouldn't matter. However, showing up in the present-day Afghanistan conflict with a musket would be a distinct disadvantage.

Besides your real job of taking care of clients, the main thing any business owner wants from IT is reliable business systems at a reasonable cost. Too often forces in the IT industry make that goal difficult to achieve.

This book provides guidance on buying technology and hiring IT support that no one else dares to publish. **The alarming and little-known fact is that the technology industry is not regulated.** Unlike other professional services, ANYONE can claim they are an "expert" with no education, training, or licensing. Further, there aren't any specific laws in existence to protect business customers – which is why it's so important for you to arm yourself with the streamlining technology secrets contained in this book.

According to the annual International Data Corporation (IDC) Profitability Report, 70% of IT service providers are not profitable and predictably fail in less than 5 years. Meanwhile, Forbes reports almost every year that it's small and midsized firms that contribute the most to the economy and have the highest demands for specialized technology expertise.

Without knowing the secrets to streamline your technology, the entire IT industry and a flawed technology strategy is working against business owners like you – unexpectedly draining cashflow and exposing you to untold risk, reputation damage, and potentially even bankruptcy. So, learn these secrets!

Message from the Author

When I wrote what became the #1 Best-Selling cybersecurity book *Easy Prey*, the reason was simple. Bad guys were using their cyber knowledge to outright rob business owners, their staff, and customers of their most precious memories and life's most important transactions.

"Revealing Secrets to Streamlining Technology" is both a little bit of revenge, but mostly giving back to the clients and the managed IT services industry. Business lessons are often the hardest you'll experience in life.

I'd worked nearly 20 years, helping people achieve so much more in less time. Just before I rose through the ranks and bought the company, my mother died and would never know I'd be CEO.

At the same time, a group of engineers stole client contracts and trade secrets for the greed of billable hours and upcharges of products. It was then that I decided I'd never sell knowledge for time or upsell commodity products.

Just like when you go to buy a car, there are so many elements stacked against you. Imagine having to deal with software you don't understand and support services that you must deal with for years.

If you can take one, or better yet 5 pearls of wisdom about streamlining technology from this book, then I've paid it forward for you and many others.

Chapter 1: Mismatched Assumptions and Motivations

"You're either making money or you're not. If you're not making money get out of the business."- Meredith Whitney

As a business owner, your real job is to grow the business. While you may be technically savvy, you have neither the time or desire to manage technology. Conventional wisdom is to hire an employee to take care of IT, have them report to accounting to control costs, and own technology instead of renting. These are outdated ideas that are diametrically opposed to your business goals.

Abdicating Authority. You make your IT employee pretty much responsible for keeping the business systems running with full access to almost everything. They must support all of your staff and any type of technology, but don't have any real authority or budget approval. Regardless, it's expected for them to document tasks, evaluate vendors, and implement multiple projects. During their personal time, IT is expected to keep up with the continual technology advancements and learn new skills. While you're on holiday or relaxing on the weekend, IT is often working and you may only vaguely notice they are still at the office during standard business hours too.

People really shouldn't wonder why so many IT folks have bad attitudes. Ask yourself how the performance of your IT is measured? When is the last time IT was provided any paid continuing education or training? What kind of strategy do you have when those responsible for IT don't know your business goals and can't evaluate return on investment, because any solution is too expensive? When was the last third-party audit of IT for your own peace of mind?

The result is three classic scenarios for IT personnel and none of them are good for your business:

1)   Build a fiefdom of more and more technology to justify hiring staff to raise their stature and require them to do less work.

2)   Learn enough new industry and technical knowledge to leverage a 10% or more increase in pay at a new employer in 1-2 years.

3)   Fly under the radar and keep legacy technology in place as long as possible until fired or retirement.

Commodity servers and software lose nearly all value immediately after purchase. Constantly hiring new technical people is highly disruptive to you, your staff, and your customers. Finally, no one wants to carry dead weight IT employees for long periods while falling behind competitors.

Dated Assumptions. The Industrial Revolution was followed by the Technological Revolution, which has given way to the current Information Revolution. You no longer need to build a waterwheel and settle by a river or lake to get drinking water. Similarly, the Federal Communications Commission (FCC) declared broadband Internet service as a utility in 2015.

The advent of cloud computing means services like e-mail and file storage are viewed in the same light. Today, the capital cost of hardware and software universally costs more than online services, with actual disadvantages for productivity and security. The hidden and more significant cost is the implementation and maintenance of on-premise systems, along with chaos for your staff and questionable protection of your customer information.

Technology Costs Rise Over Time. There's a popular myth perpetuating that the price of technology goes down over time. You can even hear it on Sirius satellite radio from Paycom about how their technology is better and more efficient, with customers never having to face a price increase. Somehow, it's not only popular to bash your competition, but never is a long time to not have a price increase or a technology glitch.

The main premise of this myth is Moore's Law and the fact that fixed costs generally decrease with more customers or transactions. Paycom is banking on new customers improving their margins more than anything about technology.

Here's why your technology costs don't go down over time:

1. **New technology demands a higher price.** Apple drops the price of iPad 2 by $100, but the new iPad Air costs as much or often more than the original price of iPad 2 because of more features or options.

2. **Competition forces new technology purchases.** Companies with old technology are perceived as offering less value by customers and employees. If the competition's sales people have new Surface tablets, then we better have something comparable or better.

3. **Technology proliferates exponentially.** In 1989 Bill Gates' goal was to have a PC on every desk and in every home. Now companies have various servers and employees have a PC, notebook, tablet, smartphone, GPS, and more.

4. **Knowledge and maintenance tend to increase.** Not only do the things you personally must know continue to increase, but the cost of specialized knowledge to keep things running continues to go up.

Bottom line. IT is likely your #4 business expense that requires management and third-party oversight. By the time you build an IT infrastructure, it's obsolete and vulnerable to attack versus having the latest technology monthly for a fraction of the cost. Finally, the rising cost of technology is as difficult to escape as death and taxes.

Chapter 2: Control Your Destiny and Avoid Capture

Seriously? How long was the staff not able to use the system and e-mail was down? How many people thought you went out of business because the website wasn't online either?

It's a common story. You wouldn't thoughtlessly give a relative stranger your power of attorney or access to your bank account. However, most business owners (large and small) regularly and naively give up full control of their reputation, communications, and business continuity. How?

Administrative Authority. The most common oversight is business owners simply not having an administrator user name and password, or even know-how to log into their own servers. Usually a terminated employee or external IT consultant is the only one who knows the password during a disaster. <u>Critical passwords and configuration details should always be accessible to management in one consolidated document called a System Plan, stored in a secure area on the system and off-site like a safe deposit box.</u>

This problem is so pervasive that at least once a week, a new client is calling because their IT support is holding them hostage. Fire anyone immediately that tries to blackmail your or hold your business hostage. If necessary, a utility may be run to reset the main administrative password and authorities may charge offenders with felony computer crimes.

Website Control. Then next blunder that is just as cataclysmic is letting random web guys control external DNS (Domain Name System). Before your eyes glaze over and you move on – PAY ATTENTION. Just like the myriad other acronyms you've learned to manage a business, this one is a definite must know.

DNS is simply the service that converts an IP address on a network or the Internet to a computer name like MY-PC or a domain name like www.matrixforce.com. If the local DNS service on a network is not working, you can't browse the Internet or send or receive e-mail. If your external DNS is not working, no one can access your network remotely, send/receive e-mail, or find your web site. Before you smugly think "I've got people who handle this for me", think again.

Do a Whois search at GoDaddy.com or any registrar by entering your domain name like matrixforce.com (without the www) and see what is displayed. For most you, the address or phone number will be wrong and some unknown vendor or past employee will be listed as contacts. Also, the renewal date is likely a shock and nowhere on your calendar reminders. If this is you, then that vendor OWNS you or if it's a past employee you must now go through a lengthy process to prove ownership.

By the way, if the DNS addresses listed at the bottom aren't related to the Registrar then you have another problem of a third-party in the mix. Which leads to the next question of where are you registered and what is the user name and password to change the information?

For best practices, you should:

1. Have your domain at a Registrar that offers not only domain creation and renewal services, but a DNS Manager and web hosting. My preference is Network Solutions (no compensation based upon this recommendation), but there is Register, Godaddy and several others. These services are long-established, stable, and reasonably priced.

2. Make your registrar account something generic, like your business name. The Registrar URL for login,

user name, and password should be kept where you can access it for maintenance and during disasters independent of a vendor, IT support, or other employee. Ideally, you should have separate contact information for the administrative and technical contacts. The e-mail address should be something generic like billing@abc.com that is associated with a distribution group or someone's actual mailbox. That way the contact isn't lost when people change roles. Plus, multiple staff can receive notices of things like pending domain name renewal to prevent website and e-mail disruption. If you want to have a technical contact for IT or a vendor, the same rule should apply using something like support@xyz.com.

3. DO NOT allow a random web guy or even an established web design company access to your Registrar account. There is a mandatory 60 day waiting period if your domain registration is moved, before you can move it back. Escaping from being captured from some no-name Registrar or web guy can be trying, because at any point they have the power to stop a transfer back. AND they don't want you to move back to someone reputable because they lose control and annual domain registration commission. Guess what? You have no e-mail or website while the transfer takes place and likely for DAYS afterwards as most web designers know little about the process and don't add any DNS settings for remote access, e-mail, or even the website.

4. DO NOT allow a random web guy or established web company to change your external DNS. To update a website, a web designer just needs is a FTP user account and password (separate from your Registrar user name and password). They desperately want to

move you to a hosting they resell, so they are motivated to not only change your web hosting but move DNS to them too. Now you're at a questionable web host for unknown long-term viability or questionable uptime. More importantly you're now totally dependent upon contacting the web design company, hoping they make any necessary changes for you. Can you say CAPTURED? Try getting ahold of Johnny-Bag-Of-Donuts during normal times, much less during that e-mail migration on the weekend or blizzard natural disaster. And yes, unless they are expert about the process and got a copy of your DNS records ahead of time to emulate at the new host, you go without e-mail and your website again.

Chapter 3: Failure to Check Requirements

The number one mistake in technology that's made continuously is failure to check requirements. It reminds me of the line "Stupid is as stupid does" from Forrest Gump. In the simple rush to help in everyday tasks or desperate struggle to finish a stalled major project, a lot of time and money is wasted with IT folks jumping into action before evaluating what is possible.

An exasperated engineer eventually gives up and calls Microsoft more than aggravated that he's spent a couple of hours updating a Windows XP desktop and then was unable to install Office 2013. Office 2013 is only supported on Windows 7 or higher and will refuse to install on anything else. Let's not even go there on why someone didn't tell you to punt and just get a new machine because Windows XP is no longer supported.

Everyone's got a similar story and for large projects, a scapegoat usually gets fired. Before you're pulled down the rabbit hole and wonder what's going on, recognize these IT blind spots:

>**Outcome**. There is usually a better way to do something in technology than your current approach. Give a full list of what you're really trying to accomplish. There is a simpler answer or your IT can provide alternatives to that perceived idea that doesn't exist yet from the movies.

>**Rules**. You know what happens when you assume. In technology, seemingly easy requests are often difficult and the complicated ask is usually a breeze. Save yourself unnecessary grief and everyone time because software and hardware manufacturers have

specifications that dictate what works together and is supported.

Stop time. The fatal flaw of virtually every technical person is that they don't know when to say when. An hour into everyday tasks is a good cut-off to stop when they're over their head or no resolution is in sight. They could have missed something or simply need to contact the manufacturer or others with more knowledge. Hopefully, they understand desired outcomes and rules above before starting that big project.

Follow the Hardware Compatibility List

Microsoft published the first Hardware Compatibility List (HCL) in 1990 for Windows 3.0. As the published article states, only the model of computers listed are certified to run Windows. The machine and ALL components must be certified as compatible by Microsoft, without any non-standard modifications.

Fast forward to today and there is a Hardware Compatibility List for every Microsoft product, along with a corresponding supported product lifecycle. Starting with Windows 10, you can even search online for an existing driver or device in the Windows Compatibility Center to verify it will work.

The technology industry grew out of hobbyist and do-it-yourself types with lots of smarts, but generally limited budget. The problem was individual hardware components like a video card may not work well with a specific motherboards or processors. To maintain quality for customers, Microsoft created the HCL so manufactures could prove their product ran well and customers could enjoy choice of the best product for whatever business application or problem they wanted to solve.

By the mid to late 90's most "clone" manufacturers of branded models of computers went out of business. Low margins and the inability to compete with large automated manufacturers were some of the biggest causes. However, the ultimate cause was the fact of poor satisfaction and quality with customers. Clone manufacturers couldn't keep up with fast changing improvements in technology and if a customer had any problems, there was no availability for support from Microsoft for the vendor or the customer.

If your hardware is not on the Microsoft Hardware Compatibility List, you have no support with Microsoft and you are responsible for diagnosing and fixing any problems.

That's why it is both alarming and fascinating that over 25 years later some service providers are beginning to put together their own clone computers. These same service providers claim that they can make better margins than reselling branded computers like Dell. Others say the pre-loaded software from major manufacturers causes too many support issues. While both arguments have some limited merit, the fact remains that customers have no support through Microsoft using any clone hardware.

Margins are so low that even IBM stopped making PCs and sold the division to the Chinese that now make Lenovo. It's highly unlikely that any service provider could sustain enough profit to build their own machines over the long run. Fortunately, public pressure has forced players like Lenovo to back off on crapware.

Following the Microsoft Hardware Compatibility List for hardware purchases is like having insurance. Your non-standard hardware may work for some period with no issues, but when something unexpected happens you want to be able to call for support.

What Does End of Support Really Mean?

Manufacturers cannot keep supporting old hardware or software and still move forward creating new and better products. It is not feasible to provide modern features for legacy software or maintain parts inventory for obsolete equipment that is no longer in demand.

Microsoft provides 10-year life cycle support on all products and Dell generally provides 3-year warranty on workstations and up to 5 years on servers. While these products may continue to function past the supported life cycle or warranty, continued usage carries a high amount of risk for security vulnerabilities and loss due to downtime.

Unfortunately, accepting such risk has stark realities for customers:

- **Additional charges.** Support provided for hardware out of warranty or software past end of life often incurs exorbitant extra fees.

- **Recovery not guaranteed.** Legacy software is usually not compatible with current applications and there are generally no replacement parts for hardware out of warranty. Besides lost productivity, the incidence of lost data increases dramatically.

- **Waterfall effect.** Unplanned emergency replacement of critical business hardware and software means an agonizing wait of days or weeks for delivery and installation. Then new hardware requires new software that complicates restoring operations and forces staff to utilize different technology with no training.

By maintaining standardization and following technology forecasts, savvy managed services customers avoid these pain points. These customers also understand that streamlining technology lowers costs and helps to improve business operations.

Chapter 4: Microsoft CSP: New Rules to Buying Software

Don't unknowingly give control of your trade secrets and employee or customer information to untrusted and unqualified entities.

How Microsoft Cloud Solution Provider (CSP) Program Affects Your Business

The war for cloud productivity and security between Google and Microsoft is over. While Google still dominates search, Microsoft has several times the subscribers for online services at a projected $20 Billion annual run rate by 2018. The challenge is now scaling to support customers.

The goal of the Microsoft Cloud Solution Provider program is to deepen customer relationships, exclusively with local Microsoft cloud champions for the best experience when moving to the cloud. Unfortunately, the minimum CSP requirements are simply providing monthly billing and technical support in a local language.

Advisor Hero

No one really knows when the cloud started. For many customers in Oklahoma, the cloud became real in 2008 with some of the worst ice storms in history. Nearly 3 million people were without power for up to two weeks and over 120,000 businesses were shutdown. Hundreds of people died with losses and damages in the billions.

2009 came with almost the same amount of devastation. This time we were ready and unlike other Sooners - our customers were largely unaffected. We had joined the fledgling Advisor Program and spent nearly a year getting certified and migrating customers to Microsoft Online Services. Over the next five years, we continued helping Oklahoma customers move their businesses ahead of the competition.

Enter Microsoft CSP

Microsoft has historically sold 90% of software and services primarily through Microsoft Partners. However, the problem with the Advisor program was that all the billing and most of the support for Microsoft Online Services was handled by Microsoft. Instead of concentrating on growing secure datacenters and improving software, torrent floods of help desk calls poured in every hour and myriad worldwide tax and billing issues occurred monthly.

Even worse, customers often needed more specialized help from partners while many partners simply collected fees under the Advisor program and gave customers the Microsoft Support number. To join in providing better customer service with a higher level of trust and competency, Matrixforce became Oklahoma's first Microsoft Cloud Solution Provider.

CSP Requirements

Unlike previous programs, only select Microsoft Partners are trusted and qualified. Although virtually all 450,000 Microsoft Partners are eligible to resell Microsoft software, the Microsoft CSP requirements are quite stringent for the protection of customers with less than 1% of Microsoft Partners being eligible.

Protect your business and ask your provider if they meet these requirements.

- C Corporation verified by the Secretary of State
- Microsoft Gold Cloud Partner listed at Microsoft Pinpoint
- Intellectual Property registered at the U.S. Patent and Trademark Office
- Annual major regulation compliance audited by third-party
- Cloud Provider contract outlining payment terms and above criteria
- Published matter expert in their competency

Go CSP

CSP is a seamless process that does not affect or interrupt your Microsoft Online Services. Go to CSP at https://matrixforce.com/csp by signing the Cloud Agreement, stopping renewal of existing services, selecting Authorize, and using your services as normal. Leverage world-class Microsoft Cloud datacenters and security combined with direct local expertise for your geography or industry, including support and billing.

In the next few years, all Microsoft software will be sold through approved distributors or Microsoft CSP partners on a subscription basis for less cost and greater security. Legacy purchase options like Open Licensing and Retail Boxes are slowing being eliminated.

Matrixforce has participated in the Microsoft Partner Network since 1994. Matrixforce is an independent Oklahoma C Corporation. Matrixforce is neither a subsidiary, nor owned by Microsoft.

Chapter 5: Rethink Your Windows 10 Strategy

WARNING: By 2020, Windows 10 will be the only operating system updated and supported by Microsoft.

Whenever a new version of Windows is released, you always hear the same things:

- Don't be on the bleeding edge.

- Stay one version behind.

- Wait until the first service pack.

- Remember Vista?

- Switch to Mac or Linux.

Then the conversation invariably turns from ugly to absurd with lines like "Microsoft has never been innovative" or "Microsoft won't be around in 5 years". You really have to wonder how many FUD (Fear Uncertainty Doubt) articles are commissioned by competitors and at what cost. Apple may dominate in the US with iPhone, but Mac has less than 5% of the market after 30 years (Source Wikipedia). Microsoft made over $4.5 Billion *after tax* per the published FY15 Q1 earnings report. The rest of the discussion quickly becomes pointless.

Except, let's ask two hard questions that will give you pause:

1. When has a new version of Windows ever been free without previously purchasing Software Assurance upgrade protection?

2. What if there were no pending service pack or next version of Windows?

Microsoft is changing the game with Windows 10. Even though there has been a long standing defined Microsoft 10-year lifecycle, the conflict has always been people resistant to change with islands of legacy software holding back major breakthroughs.

These are the top things everyone should understand about Windows 10 strategy:

Staggered Release Schedule. The official Windows 10 launch launched July 29, 2015, but only to Microsoft Insiders. There were Windows 10 Launch Celebrations worldwide, including more than 110 Microsoft Stores). Downloads for free upgrades to registered Windows 7 and 8.1 users were available through August 15, 2015. Distributors like Dell publicized models with Windows 10 for ordering availability on the official launch and have more options today. New PCs with Windows 10 arrived in retail stores like Best Buy and Wal-Mart by October 2015.

Free Windows 10 Upgrade. You must be a genuine Windows 7 SP1 or 8.1 customer to get any type of updates or upgrades. You had one year from availability to upgrade to Windows 10 for free on each device. If you didn't take advantage of the free upgrade on or before July 29, 2016, you'll have to pay $119.99 per license for Windows 10 Home and $199.99 per license for Windows 10 Pro. There was also a Windows 10 App that automatically installed on most consumer devices after applying optional updates with an offer to reserve an upgrade copy, as well as test compatibility. For business environments, the marketing was not displayed. However, Windows 10 continues to be available for download after August 15, 2015 whether you reserved a copy or not. Do not install any third-party utilities to force the Windows 10 App behavior because they are likely malicious malware.

Base Requirements. Historically, Microsoft system requirements are the bare minimum and it's no different for Windows 10 specifications. 4GB of RAM for 32-bit devices and 8GB of RAM for 64-bit devices is recommended for best performance. In general, applications that run on Windows 7 SP1 or higher will run on Windows 10. However, you should always check with the manufacturer for compatibility and test beforehand. If the hardware is older, forego the upgrade and wait until the next PC refresh.

Ring Updates. Starting with Windows 10, there will be no more Microsoft Patch Tuesday (2nd Tuesday of every month). In September 2014, Microsoft published "Windows 10 for Business" by Jim Alkove that outlined continuous security and feature updates on a slow or fast ring. The default slow ring allows administrators to configure critical security updates on demand and other feature updates one month after fast ring for the earliest scheduled updates. Under this paradigm, everyone will be on the same version of Windows going forward after upgrading to Windows 10.

Compelling Move. You'll be familiar with Windows 10 as the initial desktop and traditional Start Menu are back. Not to mention just a few features to make you more productive, like the Cortana personal assistant and new Edge browser that is 112% faster than Chrome. Just like Windows 8, you have standard built-in apps that sync across any device.

The bottom line is your applications and age of hardware will drive your decision to upgrade, but any software publisher that doesn't move to Windows 10 compatibility quickly will be far behind in the marketplace. **If you cling to the old upgrade approach of the last 20 years, the most you can delay is until Windows 7 is discontinued in 2020. By that time, what you know and use may simply be irrelevant.**

Windows 10 Privacy Conspiracy

Windows 10 privacy conspiracies rank right up there with Jade Helm and the Mayan calendar. We're being indoctrinated for martial law, doomsday has been recalculated to happen in September 2017, and Microsoft is tracking everything we do. The problem is that virtually all the controversy is simply click bait to sell more advertising from supposed "journalists" who have limited technical expertise and no experience working in the technology industry.

A good question to ask is: privacy as compared to what? Google is the company that reads your e-mail or drives down the street taking your picture. Apple is the secretive behemoth that has the largest market capitalization in the world with not one corporate blog.

Often misconstrued is the Microsoft privacy statement. No other competitor is as committed about protecting your privacy or as transparent about when Microsoft must – and arguably should comply with the law. Refresh your memories on how Microsoft has demonstrated this policy in the past.

For the first time in history, people all over the world can speak in their native language and ask the computer questions or tell it to perform tasks. Imagine verbally initiating a video call to anyone on the planet and having your speech translated. The machine learning in similar services like Focused Inbox determine your preferences and actively work to make you more productive. That's the goal versus Google who simply exists to bombard you with ads. You should at least learn the new technology, so you are not irrelevant. There are plenty of moderate approaches like turning off general options except Smart-filter in the privacy settings and simply disabling your camera/mic when not in use.

Since the Windows 10 strategy has changed to provide free upgrades and eliminate isolated islands of technology, Microsoft has chosen to try to defray some costs by offering ads in features like the new Edge browser. These ads can be easily turned off while surfing the web or during other uses by accessing the Microsoft Personalized Ad Preferences to opt out. For business users, it's recommended to setup a Microsoft Account using your business e-mail so you can separate work and home or personal devices and uses.

We all need to be vigilant to protect our freedoms, while analyzing the source of information and respecting the rights of others. Otherwise, you encourage hysteria and there will assuredly be many conspiracy theories always looming in future.

Chapter 6: Cheapest Way to Buy Microsoft Office

One of the more common requests we get are for quotes on Microsoft Office. The usual reasons are:

- Our version of Office is no longer supported or doesn't work with other software

- There is no standardization causing confusion and productivity loss for employees

- We're having problems converting or opening newer Microsoft Office documents

Hands down Office 365 is the best way to purchase Microsoft Office, either separately or bundled subscriptions like Office 365 E3. This approach is the most cost-effective and provides an **always current version of Microsoft Office for up to 5 devices per user:**

Office 365 Enterprise E3 ($240 per user per year)

Office 365 Pro Plus ($144 per user per year)

Let's take a typical scenario of an organization with 100 users and a mixture of Office 2003, Office 2007, and Office 2010. You basically have 4 purchase options:

1. Retail boxes from a retailer like Best Buy ($399.99)

2. Open license from a distributor ($508)

3. Open license with Software Assurance upgrade protection ($803)

4. Office 365 subscription that includes Office (starting at $144 per year)

Note: Microsoft Open License Estimated Retail Price List is published publicly.

Retail boxes are difficult to manage with the separate keys for each license and cost nearly 3 times an Office 365 subscription with no upgrade protection. Similarly, an Open License is approximately 4 times the cost of an Office 365 subscription and no upgrade protection.

Given the rapid pace of technology only increasing, it's unlikely that you can wait 4 or 5 years to upgrade any more. Open Licenses with Software Assurance make no sense with a 2 or 3-year renewal, at almost 6 times the cost for the same upgrade protection provided in Office 365.

So, the choice boils down to buying Open licenses you own versus renting a monthly Office 365 Subscription:

> **$50,800** – Office Professional Pro Plus for 100 Users Open License

> **$14,400** – Office 365 Pro Plus for 100 Users per year

Office 365 is only a fraction of the cost annually for 5 times the value. Be a hero with your stockholders and show them the cheapest way to buy Microsoft Office.

Only Office 365 ProPlus Approved for Microsoft Online Services

On February 28, 2017, Microsoft announced support was ending for Office 2013. This marks a striking new change, as previously Microsoft supported the previous and current versions of Office for download and use with Office 365 and other Microsoft Online Services.

Also, quietly reported and less publicized was the report that sometime in the fall of 2017, Open License and Retail versions of Microsoft Office Professional 2016 or earlier may not connect to Office 365. Just like Windows 10, Microsoft Office will perpetually be updated for one supported version so all users can enjoy the latest productivity and highest security features.

Chapter 7: Azure Top 10 Important Buying Tips

In April of 2014, Microsoft News reported that Office 365 had reached a $2.5 billion annual revenue rate. Since that time, the usage of all Microsoft Online Services has continued to accelerate with growing interest and confusion about Microsoft Azure. The following points provide some insight for customers to avoid pitfalls and better understand how to leverage this technology:

1. **Azure is a platform and not a specific product or service.** All Microsoft Online Services including Office 365 are run on Azure. In addition, Microsoft Azure features include:

    1. **Compute:** virtual machines, cloud services, parallel and batch compute jobs, and RemoteApps.

    2. **Web & Mobile:** web apps, mobile apps, logic apps, API apps, notification hubs, and mobile engagement.

    3. **Data & Storage:** SQL database, DocmentDB, Redis Cache, StorSimple, and Azure search.

    4. **Analytics & Internet of Things:** HDInsight, machine learning, stream analytics, data factor, event hubs, and SQL data warehouse.

    5. **Networking:** virtual network, ExpressRoute, Traffic Manager, load balancing, DNS, and VPN gateway.

    6. **Media and CDN:** Media services, encoding, Azure Media Player, media intelligence, content

protection, live and on-demand streaming, and CDN.

7. **Hybrid Integration:** BizTalk services, service bus, backup, and site recovery.

8. **Identity and Access Management:** Azure Active Directory and multi-factor authentication.

9. **Developer Services:** Visual Studio Online and Visual Studio Application Insights.

10. **Management:** preview portal, scheduler, automation, operational insights, and key vault.

2. **The most popular services are AD Connect, Site Recovery, RemoteApp, and Virtual Machines.**

    1. **AD Connect:** Allows customers to have the same password for the network and Microsoft Online Services.

    2. **Site Recovery:** Replicates offline copies of on premise virtual machines for disaster recovery.

    3. **RemoteApp:** Provides the capability to publish popular applications like QuickBooks accessible from any device without a VPN or managing a virtual server.

    4. **Virtual Machines:** Traditional Windows or Linux virtual servers hosted at Microsoft rather than on premise.

3. **A firewall that supports dynamic VPN is required in a hybrid environment.** For a hybrid environment, a site to site VPN must be established to Microsoft with a firewall that supports dynamic VPN. Lower-end firewalls like some SonicWALL models support dynamic VPN, but may not be robust enough for throughput while higher-end Cisco firewalls oddly do

not support this feature. Matrixforce recommends and supports only Fortinet firewalls for Azure connections.

4. **Understanding Azure account setup is very important.** Your Azure subscription should be created using a Microsoft Account for flexibility and avoiding limitations with an organizational account. The initial logon created becomes the service and account administrator for the Azure subscription. The account administrator cannot be changed and controls the account portal for Azure, which is managed separately from the Management Portal using the service administrator account. Best practice is to use the same account for both roles and create co-administrator accounts for the management portal as needed.

5. **Azure may be purchased via credit card, Open License Azure credits, or Azure Enterprise Agreement.** The simplest, but most expensive way to purchase Azure services is by credit card. Azure Enterprise Agreements are intended for large customers with high usage scenarios. Open License is the preferred method to purchase Azure. Open Licenses provide a key to apply toward a single subscription for the purchased amount of credits (approximately $100 each). Open License credits must be activated within 5 years after purchase or become void. Once activated, the credits are only valid for one year whether consumed by services or not. Open License orders typically take 24-72 hours to process, so it is imperative to monitor usage to prevent downtime. Unfortunately, very few people in the channel understand these rules or can explain them to customers.

6. **Support is not included and billed separately.** The only support you automatically receive for Azure is free billing or account questions. For any technical support, you must purchase an Azure support plan.

7. **Usage or consumption is difficult to estimate.** ADConnect and low traffic websites are free. However, we challenge any rocket scientist to pick a business scenario and then confidently calculate usage cost using the Azure Price Calculator. Some services are flat cost and others are billed by the hour or gigabyte. You can upload data for free, but data egress or download incurs a charge. Fortunately, the calculated pricing is usually higher than reality. However, the only way to truly understand billing is testing usage or working with an experienced vendor.

8. **Azure subscription payment types cannot be changed.** If you have a trial backed by a credit card and want to buy some Open License Azure Credits, then you'll have to create a new Microsoft Account and a new Azure subscription. Then you must contact Azure billing support to transfer applications and data to your new Azure account.

9. **Transition of services from one Azure subscription to another is not seamless.** Although transition is free, not everything is transferred and accounts with any significant amount of data may take 24 -72 hours. Any advanced services like RemoteApp and even common requirements like Active Directory must be moved by you manually.

10. **Don't buy Azure, but rather services from a qualified Microsoft Cloud Partner.** Less than 1% of Microsoft Partners are qualified to conduct business or configure Azure services, but they will gladly sell Open License Azure credits for a small commission. However, once you buy Azure credits, you then have to figure everything else out and purchase support. A better alternative is to leverage the technology, while mitigating the risk and complexity by purchasing offerings like

RemoteApp or virtual machines for a flat cost per month with support from a qualified partner like Matrixforce.

Microsoft Azure provides enormous benefits to businesses by lowering the burden of uptime and disaster recovery for most current technology. However, it is key to understand the right way to purchase and configure to avoid costly transitions and disruptions to business. Matrixforce is a top 100 provider of Microsoft Online Services today and anticipates 80% of cloud customers utilizing some form of Azure in the next 5 years.

Chapter 8: Trade Secret Proposal Tips

Whether you're a customer or a vendor, there are many undisclosed facts about proposals. The most protected truth is that the decision is already made and the game is rigged before a proposal is ever presented. As a Virtual CIO for the last 20 years, I've had the benefit of being on both sides – helping customers identify requirements and pitching solutions as a service provider. Unfortunately, no one can be told the realities of modern buying and selling transactions for technology solutions because you have to truly experience them for yourself.

> *You know something is not right during the process. You can't explain it, but it feels wrong. Beware, as this is your last chance. You can stop now and go back to believing whatever you want or you can continue and see how far the rabbit hole goes.*

Commerce began centuries ago, when people bartered supplies to live – which eventually evolved into various forms of money for any conceivable good or service. Less than 100 years ago, magical machines like the computer were invented, based upon abstract ideas for virtually any use. Software and other intangibles that you couldn't really touch or quantify entered the marketplace. No one really knows when the first technology proposal was created. There was no other way to explain the concepts and value. What we do know is that we've been a slave to the process ever since.

Buyer Proposal Guidance

For the last decade, customers have overwhelming had the upper hand using the Internet to gather information. The problem is the use of supposed "conventions" from generations ago or general laziness prevents getting the best solution or hiring the best service provider. Customers don't ask the right questions when first meeting a prospective service provider or reseller, much less avoid even bigger mistakes going forward.

Request for Proposal Debacle. What seems obvious in business is seldom the case and Request for Proposals (RFPs) are no exception. Internally, there is always a member of the team that has an agenda to steer to their favorite vendor. Also, isn't it funny that the company that helps put together the requirements almost always wins the bid? The reason is certain aspects that only one vendor can fulfill are slipped into the requirements. Seasoned industry players readily recognize competitor traits and know the RFP game too, and simply refuse to respond if there was no involvement with creating the RFP. To fill out the perfunctory 3 bids, only startups not familiar with the process will quote or wily vendors that seek to change the requirements in their favor during the process.

The other factor customers don't even consider is that the technology industry has grown so fast, that it has matured in a few decades versus centuries for other industries. For hundreds of years, major shipping companies in Europe bludgeoned each other competing on trade routes, until one day the two top shipping firms formed a secret alliance to share information and decide who got the business. Technology firms belong to various industry associations with such arrangements decided long ago. Don't assume you're a savvy customer and are ahead of the game, because you're habits and initiatives are likely known by many vendors who don't even do business with you.

Customers should be able to gather their own requirements or use a vendor to help that is not eligible to bid. Today, pricing for solutions is readily available on the web including cost calculators for services. Ditch the RFP, identify your needs with an idea of cost, and then pick your two favorite candidates to submit a proposal. Save everyone the time and agony. Besides, you never consider the third bidder anyway.

Deal Registration Trap. In World War II, the U.S. had a propaganda campaign of "loose lips sink ships" for servicemen and citizens to avoid unguarded talk. This concept is an important lesson for buyers as well. When a customer asks any vendor for a quote, it's likely they've unknowingly triggered a deal registration. Most hardware and software manufacturers have a deal registration process to identify potential customers and assign the reseller. The twist is that the assigned reseller then owns the opportunity and has the best discount, with other resellers often prevented from getting a quote from the manufacturer. Often when a customer contacts a manufacturer directly, the manufacturer may lock out any resellers to win a deal at the highest margin.

For hardware, the manufacturer has the best price for ordinary purchases and the reseller has more discount for high-end or specialty items. For software, the pricing is often controlled and only available through assigned partners. Major software distributors may have year-end rebates that allow loss leader pricing on certain items to charge the highest margin on products under deal registration. Understanding this process is just more rationale why customers shouldn't recklessly solicit quotes from any part of the sales channel.

Qualification Failure. While mysteries like deal registration may be a revelation, many customers fail to properly analyze proposals or truly qualify a vendor. Let's face it. Most proposals are 90% irrelevant or "puffing" noise. However, besides the numbers, the two areas that should be scrutinized heavily are background and terms.

For professional technology services, customers should only hire C Corporations with listed ownership by the Secretary of State. Otherwise, you don't really know if you're dealing with a foreign entity, gambling venture capitalists, potential competitors, felonious individuals, or any other unwanted associations. It's great if the vendor has 85 people, but it doesn't mean much if they are all web developers and you need infrastructure support. Always visit the local office and at least have a conference call with the vendor's board.

Like license agreements or website terms, most customers blow by the fine print in proposals. Invariably, rights are waived for any recourse or liability for equipment and risk is transferred to the customer with heavy penalties. All of these red flags are when customers should not negotiate, but walk away and start over.

Seller Proposal Guidance

While customers may not really know the game, it's the vendors presenting proposals that are really lost. The whole sales process is generally a hot mess and shows by the time a proposal is presented. Panicked sales people trying to make quota and get paid only really know bluster or deception. The proposals generally mirror this stance with additional irrelevant information as padding to seem more authoritative.

Proposal Dilemma. Here's the stark reality. Most IT service providers and resellers offer nothing unique or impactful. Further, compensation models are generally not aligned with firm goals to help customers (usually not a concern either). Without any true specialization, customers often decide the cost of doing nothing is less than randomly picking a vendor from a pack of mediocre clone responses.

Up your standards and provide a better offering. If a competitor regularly dominates you in the marketplace, it's because they have a better strategy. Proposals should not have 10-30 pages of overwhelming detail, but rather succinct solutions with a financial approach. Endless comparisons, frequent questions, options, and related preferences should be discussed well before presenting a proposal. An overhaul of flawed marketing and sales process develops better proposals and customer buying experience.

Customer focus. The standard proposal formula is all about the vendor: background, current statistics, facilities, press, and latest awards. Throw in some specifications flyers with pricing and a terrible impression is assured. Instead, how about describing the customer pain and showing the process of how you can help in graphical form, along with a timeline? Also, include caveats so the customer has no unknown surprises. If the customer doesn't know your story and value by the time a proposal is presented, then you have no chance of winning anyway.

Are you a technology service provider or reseller and think you're different? Take a few minutes and compare competitive websites in dismay at the similarities. Likewise, stop the foolish and indefensible statements in proposals: leading company, state-of-the-art, best of breed, full service, fast growing, and trustworthy. Why continue to damage your credibility?

Proper presentation. Don't tell anyone, but do you know the most colossal proposal mistake? Well it's naïve technologists or cowardly sales people who blindly e-mail a proposal and then wonder why the customer won't call back or speak to them.

Imagine if your doctor mailed some x-rays and a big bill without identifying the break or explaining the prognosis. Review proposals with customers personally. The concept may seem like common sense, but few vendors get it. Customers who refuse to meet for proposal review aren't serious about buying either.

Hopefully, the secrets revealed above help you to avoid some pitfalls and improve your approach. Everyone wins with better evaluation and quicker transactions.

Chapter 9: Navigating the IBM Sales Approach

Over the years, I've seen just about every sales approach from half a dozen industries – some I've even tried myself. While we abandoned it in the early 90's, the IBM sales approach is still popular in the technology industry today.

To be clear, there is nothing wrong with the approach and no derision toward IBM is intended. However, from the customer's perspective, it's rather daunting and prompts decisions you wouldn't normally make.

One of my customers contacted me about some technology they were considering. After asking what they were trying to accomplish, the customer was starting from near zero on comprehension. I did a quick demo of some similar technology to show some concepts and sent an industry cost comparison of different products. He then asked if I could be there next week for the presentation.

We had some other business, so I arrived an hour early. To my customer's surprise and mine, a team of three people showed up a half hour early. When you're traveling some distance, that might be ok. However, coming from two miles away and arriving so early is disruptive by design.

In hand, they had brought a dozen fancy donuts, along with a dozen sausage rolls. Even though you have a process, nothing beats preparation and research. The customer had some health issues and had just spent the last 9 months losing over 150 pounds. It was apparently a hungry sales team in more ways than one, as they proceeded to eat when no one else did during the presentation.

The approach using three people is meant to convey size and credibility of the company. When meeting with one or two people, it's an overwhelming show of force. In this case it was three on three, so it didn't matter.

There was the remote access guru, the storage expert, and the licensing whiz. After some brief preliminaries, the discussion was lively from the full gamut of virtually every technology. Here's all of these features, you probably really need a SAN (even though that was never previously mentioned), and sometimes the software was licensed per user or by bundle.

Finally, I said "please draw a picture on the board". Then some real business questions and answers happened. The guru even showed a couple of examples on his iPad. Shortly thereafter, the customer asked for a couple of quotes and the team left. The quote would apparently come in two days. Oddly, no one inquired about the timing of the project which was in 6 months.

Based upon the example on the white board, the customer was floored by the layers of software and the complexity. The solution seemed like it would be significant cost as well.

Afterwards, I showed the customer what we used for remote access. He opened a file from a drive mapping and printed to a local printer using his own workstation. These were the bulk of his requirements and customer had lots of straight-forward choices.

The technology the vendor described and eventually showed was indeed "slick". Nonetheless, it was a wrecking ball when a hammer was all that was required. Worse yet, the maintenance and upgrades were the significant dollars. Here are the quick tips for navigating the IBM sales approach:

1. Expect some psychology game. The vendor arriving inordinately early with three or more people and a plethora of geek speak.

2. Do your own research. Try to have a good sense of the results you are trying to achieve. Go to the vendor's website. Compare competing product features, pricing, and case studies.

3. Ask for a picture. It does provide a thousand words and hopefully fills in the blanks, especially along with demos.

4. Avoid the embrace and extend. While it may sound good, get the quotes to evaluate and then eliminate the "extras".

This sales team didn't appear green, but were obviously rushed and did little preparation. Customers should expect some qualifying questions upfront. Even for small Office 365 deals, I will:

- Call the customer before we meet to get an understanding of need and timeframe
- Connect with them on LinkedIn to see background
- Research their website and competitors for industry requirements
- Lookup MX records, domain registration, ISP, and current e-mail system

The landscape has changed greatly over the years for buying and selling because of the Internet. If either buyer or seller comes into the situation unprepared, it's an obvious warning sign. If a customer is unprepared, then they may inadvertently succumb to the legacy IBM sales approach.

Chapter 10: Washing Machine Syndrome

At some point in your life, it happens. The washing machine stops spinning out or simply dies. What a major inconvenience to have wet and soapy clothes. You may have to go buy some underwear for the next couple of days or try to find a laundromat. It costs as much to repair as it does to buy a replacement. If you're fortunate, you whip out the credit card on the weekend and try not to get sucked into your favorite color or cool front loader with the matching new dryer. Depending upon your stage in life, you may be forced to hit the garage sales and get a friend with a truck to pick one up.

Regardless, the old washing machine is removed and the new one plugged in and screwed to the hot and cold water. You're back in business and wash away without another thought, until it happens again in another 6-8 years. The problem is that many companies take the same approach with their servers and it's definitely not as simple as replacing the washing machine.

Anyone in business can tell you, there is significant risk and lots of small and massive failures. Owners have a lot of moving pieces to understand and must have the courage to make decisions like that old Kenny Rogers song – count your money, be ready for the cards you are dealt, and know when to walk away or run. These same people wouldn't dare try to not pay payroll tax for a couple of months (which can never be escaped), but regularly risk it all to run 12 – 36 months out of warranty on servers running the business.

You see I have a unique ability to tell the future about when a server will die. Well, actually it's simple. Servers are generally warranted for 3 years with some limited options for upfront 4 or 5 years. That means there are no parts or extremely limited spare refurbished parts throughout the world at warranty end – thank you lean manufacturing. So that means if you have only one power supply that shorts out, it's 5-10 business days to have a new server shipped, plus emergency recovery because complex hardware and software just isn't like plugging in a new washing machine.

Bad RAM, that old type is probably not available. If you have RAID and one drive dies and the machine is still running, try 5 times the cost of a new one with 5 times the capacity wasted to replace.

I've heard it all: "That's the best server we ever bought" or "We just got that server in 2012". This is generally begun or ended with some explicative or irrational statement about so much was spent, it should last for 20 years. Then, wait for it, the new equipment won't run any of the old software and the new software requires other new software.

Treating your infrastructure like a washing machine just costs the business half to a full month's expenses and revenues, in addition to lost goodwill with employees, customers, and suppliers – along with bad press and loss of new potential sales. But it's IT or that support firm's fault right? We'll just fire those bastards. After all, IT has no budget authority, those consultants were crazy, and the recruiter of the day with PC Magazine says anybody can do this stuff.

While it may feel good to fire someone in this situation, how about trying to prevent it in the future? Fact: your equipment is only as good as the warranty. Often, it's only $200 – $400 more to get that 4-hour 4-year warranty part replacement from Dell. Then a hardware problem is fixed quickly versus doing everything by hand, waiting 10 business days for a new server, and weeks to workout restoration with the waterfall effect of upgraded software.

Back in the day like 10 years ago, the answer was to buy two of each server or a spare parts kit for each server. The cost was exorbitant and the software configuration overly complex and rarely worked. Nowadays, you stop repeating the washing machine syndrome by:

1. **Cloud Computing** – Get rid of most of your servers. Escape the cost of hardware, software, maintenance, and upgrades. Along with less cost, a big chunk of your disaster recovery is also resolved.

2. **Virtualization** – What servers are left should be virtual with reduced equipment cost and the side benefit of running on older versions of software on the virtual servers longer.

3. **Managed IT Services** – You've outsourced everything from the coffee service to payroll, because those services do it better and for less cost. Why not shrink or eliminate your IT staff for the same benefits? The best service providers manage cloud computing and virtualization, as well as keeping you current for anything on-premise.

Chapter 11: What to Pay for IT Support

Baseline cost for determining IT support can be researched at the Bureau of Labor Statistics for staffing or outsourcing.

Most employers and technology employees are out of touch with current technology trends or changes in required staffing and associated compensation. The trend is fewer IT people per employer, along with shrinking technology infrastructure due to cloud computing and offerings like Virtual CIO and Managed IT Services.

While every major staffing firm or industry trade magazine has a salary guide, the problem is that sample size is small and the participants and publishers have a vested interest in making sure the salaries are high with no verification of real wages.

The right way to determine what to pay and expect for a position is listed at the U.S. Bureau of Labor Statistics (BLS) by state. The following shows the average pay for individuals with 7-10 years of experience in Oklahoma (as a national median):

Position	# Jobs	Mean	Hourly
Network Administrator	2,500	$67,690	$32.55
Computer Network Specialist	1,270	$59,940	$28.22
Computer Support Specialist	7,070	$43,370	$20.85

You can verify this information and check other **Computer and mathematical** positions for Oklahoma at the BLS. These figures do not include bonuses or benefits such as healthcare and individuals job duties with the above titles often varies drastically. In Oklahoma and throughout the nation, the technology industry is schizophrenic with some very good people making low wages and nominally skilled ones raking in above average salaries. Because it is a competitive industry, most employers find it difficult to retain technical employees over 3 years – the vast majority of employers provide no training, measurement of performance, management, or significant room for advancement to technology employees.

For the reasons above and given the average added cost of 30% for taxes and benefits, most employers under 300 employees are electing to outsource technology support to a managed IT service provider.

Hire, Contract or Outsource?

Every business today faces the same dilemma for Information Technology: hire an employee, short-term contractor, or managed IT service. There are specific scenarios for each choice.

While the common misconception is that hiring an IT employee is the safest and easiest to control, the reality is that hiring an IT employee is generally the highest cost and risk. Consider that employers pay 22% on top of employee salary for taxes alone. Once you add benefits and management oversight, the up-charge is often more than salary + 30%. Due to the competitive nature of the industry, IT personnel generally change jobs every 2 years keeping employers in constant flux. Finally, even though IT employees have extraordinary access to business information, most employers haven't begun to consider how to measure IT performance, motivate, or understand the IT role.

An IT department's main charge is keeping systems running and responding to users. Implementation of new technology is often done by a contractor. Projects may be easily defined and corresponding spend/return readily measured. Project work is not for the faint of heart and using contractors has moderate cost and risk due to the inherent up and down nature of demand. Most one-man shops have been decimated and the best approach is to contract with a company that regularly implements similar projects or a staffing firm to locate an individual.

Managed IT services are the best value for cost and low risk. As usual, you should avoid limited liability firms that are less than 10 years old identified by only offering some limited monitoring and no project implementation. Ideally, the managed service firm you pick should include business consulting, guaranteed response, and flat cost for support and projects. **You should save a minimum of 30% – 40% versus an IT staff and 15% – 20% on projects. Most businesses keep one IT person to focus on higher end issues to move the company forward and as a liaison for users.**

Flat Cost vs Billable Hours

We Sooners are known for first to fight or aid for wars and disasters. Given the auspicious start for our state, we're also a bold and stubborn lot that unfortunately trails the nation in business trends and technology. For over 30 years, our firm has provided flat cost professional services for IT. This decision was obviously a business strategy and my former partner often said "I've made enough mistakes in business that would have paid for dozens of college degrees". (By the way, I'm proud to report that he is neither dead or estranged and was simply bought out on amicable terms in 2003.)

While most of the industry eliminated the billable hour over a decade ago, much of the state channel still utilize billable hours which are bad for customers because it is fraught with conflict, deception, and poor performance. The conflict is often heated before, during, and after projects for rate and number of hours. Critical tasks may be shortened or eliminated imposing significant risk and costing additional time resulting in significant overage – which leads to the main deception of padding hours to start or milking tasks during. When you pay by the hour, the only incentive is to stick around and bill more hours. Forget about thoroughness, prevention of future problems, or anything relating to efficiency and quality.

Flat cost is a win-win for customers and professional managed IT services firms. Customers know what they're paying and service providers leverage their expertise and assume all of the risk for the unforeseen and lengthier than expected engagements. However, we occasionally still have prospects ask things like "How can I compare without hours?"

And there it is: a descriptive list of tasks/outcomes, estimated due date, and total cost. Now you compare approach, credibility, and repeat wins. No it's not fair to startups or one-man-shows with their journeyman approach of rate and hours, desperate hope of impressing with the 10 page brochure website, and Better Business Bureau (BBB) logo everywhere even though no focus on consumers. Comparison is done on business criteria rather than the sales person who was liked the most, along with the hourly company the CFO feels is easiest to renegotiate or delay payment based upon too many hours.

Obviously, the more physical or smaller the task may make time and charges a better fit (like cabling). However, for the viability of a business, achieving goals with smooth operation is often a much more valued criterion than simply cost. Again, we sometimes hear "You obviously started with hours so why not show them?"

It's MBA 101 and anyone doing pricing knows cost-plus is easy to understand and manipulate, but also a novice business approach that has diminishing growth potential leading to eventual bankruptcy. It comes down to business savvy and motivation. If we haven't proven our worth upfront and will not make a required margin, then it's not a fit for either us or the customer. Our personnel are not paid by the hour, so the only motivation is providing good service and not dragging out every task to make the weekly hourly bonus.

Chapter 12: Scorecard to Measure IT

Accountability can be a tough word, just like fulfillment. I'm often amazed when I ask a client how is your performance measured and what's your daily routine? Maybe it's because they think we're going to immediately talk about systems, or hardware and software inventory, or some technology concept they don't care to understand.

My clients are midsized organizations that either struggle mightily with technology or have competent IT staff and want to learn what they can do better. Both types want to move to the next level and are either desperate or smart enough to have realized they can't continue to do things the same old way.

When I speak with someone in IT, it's generally the same story over and over. Performance is measured by some vague notion of if the staff seems happy and uptime of the network. There are no real measurements and most people only remember the occasional bad stuff. Even though these IT folks have great responsibility and access, they don't have: a budget, training, or any real authority. Every day is just another fire drill or the same menial tasks.

For owner's or members of operations, you would think that I had sucker-punched them in the nose. There's a look of astonishment as they might have a notion of what a Job Scorecard is, but have not put it together and analyzed the things they do on a daily, monthly, or annual basis. For these management teams, it's very common for them to suddenly realize all their time spent on e-mail is a huge disconnect from customers, while most other remaining tasks are meaningless in helping the firm grow too. When you point out that they have no strategy for information technology, it's a painful awakening that the number four business expense has largely been ignored

– not to mention security, business continuity, productivity, or competitive advantage.

The general approach is to shove technology under the responsibility of the Chief Financial Officer. The main thought is to control costs. However, there is no technology vision or expertise. Both mundane and dire technology situations are all handled reactively with the IT personnel supposed to just "handle it" with no budget, know how, or authority. "Oh by the way, we have to keep business running", so in addition to your normal schedule you'll work nights, weekends, and holidays as needed too while the rest of the staff is off. Now you can understand why so many IT people have poor attitudes.

Invariably something is down, data is lost, or there is a major security breach. Revenues are lost as contracts are broken and brands are damaged due to bad publicity. Severity of these problems is generally based upon: lack of controls, documentation, and education. The three biggest complaints and fears that midsized businesses have are:

1. They don't know what IT does, struggle with oversight, and worry about risk and reliability.

2. They are held hostage as little is documented or tested for any type of business continuity situation.

3. They know both their IT and staff are lacking basic knowledge keeping the firm less productive

In his best-selling book *Scaling Up*, Verne Harnish outlines several organizational ideas including the One Page Plan (OPP) and the Job Scorecard. The OPP is a useful drill for anyone in operations or management to analyze what is unimportant and they should stop doing, as well as truly important tasks to help the business grow and start doing. You also get to account for family, faith, and friends. The biggest improvement is often adjusting to a better email paradigm shift.

The next major improvement is giving some true accountability to IT (and possibly the rest of the staff) by eliminating old job descriptions and corresponding verbose and mostly pointless annual review reports. When clients do their first Job Scorecard for IT, they quickly realize they don't have enough staff, tools, or budget to achieve the accountability required for the firm's strategy.

Many clients have never considered a scorecard for IT and often don't have a monitoring tool or case management system. Further IT has no time to document anything or perform server maintenance, between responding to user issues and struggling to complete projects. Many clients decide to implement managed services, since there is no budget to hire more IT staff or build and maintain new business systems. For half the cost of a full-time employee, the network can be monitored and documented with audited oversight for IT and proven business strategies going forward. Unnecessary costs are eliminated and IT personnel can focus on helping end-users and strategic initiatives for management.

Once scorecards are implemented, the ABC scoring for reviews is short and simple. True measurements are available for performance with employees better informed and more productive. Best of all, the IT staff does more meaningful work, while putting in fewer hours and helping the firm do more business.

www.matrixforce.com

Job Scorecard

Job Title: IT Support Specialist
Department: Support
Reports To: Practice Manager
Modified Date: December 13, 2014

Mission

The core mission of an IT Support Specialist is managing and implementing strategies to streamline technology for medium business clients. Support specialists are expected to respond to client requests promptly, follow-up regularly, proactively resolve errors, document and improve repetitive tasks, and implement projects to reduce complexity and improve operations. Support Specialists configure and troubleshoot cloud, virtual, and physical hardware and software systems; provide technical assistance and training to system users; and update knowledgebase and Standard Operating Procedures.

Accountability

Description	Metric	Rating (A,B,C)	Comments
Retain Accounts	Provide outstanding support with a 4-person team to retain assigned clients		
Projects	10 projects completed annually using Delta methodology		
Documentation	12 standard operating procedures or blog posts annually and system plan update with each project		
Activity / Competency	Follow-up and cases completed daily. Project completion within 15 days. Annual compliance training & 1-2 Certification or CPE events as needed.		

Competency

- Courteous & humble
- Superior communication
- Client empathy
- Strong time management
- Analytical reasoning
- Results oriented
- Resourceful & proactive

- Windows & Windows Server
- Active Directory
- Exchange and SQL
- Remote Desktop and Virtualization
- Networking and firewalls
- Microsoft Online Services
- Dell desktop, servers, and storage

BS/BA or 2-3 years of experience required with annual background check. A personal smartphone and home computer with Internet access is expected, as well as a valid driver's license/insurance and ability to lift or move a PC. Reasonable accommodations may be made for individuals with disabilities.

Chapter 13: Pinpoint Your Vector Growth Phase

36 months is the average cyclical timeframe for information technology to continually go from chaos to smooth operations – another 24 months for competitive advantage.

The majority of business owners get stuck in a rut or stopped by some imaginary glass ceiling. The main underlying reason is often because their approach to IT is hindering all other operations and departments. For this reason, the Fream Vector Growth Model was created to show business leaders where they are in technology maturity and how to move business forward.

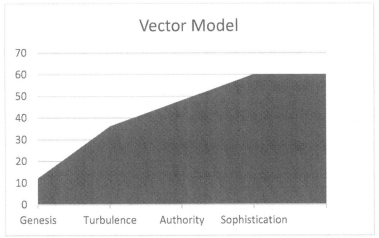

Source: streamliningtechnology.com

Genesis. The beginning stage is implementing technology solutions based upon reduced complexity, rather than by the budget of technical features. The concept starts with an initial understanding that some services are recommended to be outsourced at a far less cost with greater productivity and security than any do-it-yourself approaches, which may misleadingly seem more cost effective.

A good example is moving e-mail to the cloud with Office 365 for a fraction of running your own e-mail server with the high capital cost and on-going maintenance with far less security.

Turbulence. The following step is where management begins to take a lead role in fully understanding technology strategy and implementation, as opposed to abdicating leadership to the accounting or technology personnel within a company. The result is old paradigms of support and purchasing are both challenged and streamlined.

A simple overview diagram provides a quick picture of your IT. Costs become predictable with a 5-year technology forecast based upon hardware warranty and software support renewal. Add a regular system health Executive Summary with quarterly project status and management teams can now look for opportunities to improve operations.

"70% of companies fail to transition from Turbulence to Authority"

Authority. Critical IT infrastructure services are consolidated and therefore the risk is distributed across a smaller number of products and services. The organization then begins publishing intellectual property as a differentiator in being both more trustworthy than their competitors and offering more value for customers.

Removing disruption from employees allows them to focus on customers and provide valuable tips to customers for retention and new sales. Because employees do nearly as much work out of the office as inside the office, the medieval castle approach of multiple layers of security is useless and outrageously expensive in present day. Cloud services like Microsoft Enterprise Mobility Suite offer Microsoft Updates, third-party updates like Java and Adobe, and remote lock / restart / wipe capabilities for 5 devices per user and at less cost than legacy anti-virus alone.

Sophistication. The last phase entails the organization evaluating their return on investment, while continuing to focus on better customer experience. Special emphasis by management is taken in reviewing processes for any business improvement with the consideration of new technology.

Standard Operating Procedures (SOPs) may be developed for operations to minimize staff changes and improve customers service. Calculated risks may be taken to choose what projects to start or delay based upon known information rather than guessing. For instance, the cost of customer acquisition is calculated and the cost and effective implementation of marketing campaigns can now be measured.

Once you identify the current operational stage of technology within your organization, you have a better understanding of weaknesses. Therefore, you can begin to evaluate a breakeven between technology costs and business improvement versus the risk of reputation damage and compliance penalties. Unfortunately, an estimated seventy percent of businesses are so resistant to change that they never make it past the Turbulence stage. As evidenced by research every few years by Forbes and Bloomberg, this obstinate lot eventually fails in their endeavors. Industry forces like unexpected ransomware, data breach, negative publicity, lost revenue just hasten the demise.

Chapter 14: Digital Marketing for More Customers

If you look at a typical sales funnel today, digital marketing has already educated customers and helped them make decisions well before talking to sales. In fact, virtually everything in traditional sales is equally despised and ineffectual. The only real way to get more customers in the current marketplace is to have better digital marketing.

The problem is that people have so much information overload. Recent studies show we have the 7 second attention span of a gold-fish. You need a better strategy to attract your ideal customer when they are ready to buy.

We all have a story of how the business was started. It is the genesis of how we've triumphed and endured. Add your beliefs about service and you have a direct message to connect with your best prospects. Telling stories is a difficult skill to master, but you get better with practice and are infinitely more interesting.

Rank your best customers and discover your secret sauce to Pumpkin Plan Your Marketing (pumpkinplan.com). When you figure out the immutable laws that make your organization different and draw the very customers you love, then you have a roadmap for a better value proposition AND more notice in the marketplace. It's not an easy drill and quite painful to realize how much time you've wasted doing things that don't matter to you or your dream customer.

The average business spends less than $1 per customer on each marketing transaction. One of our industry's leading mentors, Robin Robins, has a great line she regularly uses: "E-mails are like toots in the wind." Good marketers today have customers coming to them and spend $35 per customer interaction with things like a Shock-and-Awe box. Common content may include: video, book, case study, special report, and industry comparison. Using this approach, customers get that you know what you're doing and receive something of value regardless of whether you do business. Put another way, they trust what you say and you both can have a business discussion. Quickly understanding what each other does and qualifying or disqualifying a fit is a win for everyone.

Obviously, your website is a key asset for your marketing. However, the world recently changed dramatically when Google announced SSL encryption for better search ranking. Not only are potential customers put off by your lack of security, but you're unwittingly letting competitors track your keywords too.

Likewise, in breaking news, Mobilegeddon has happened and who cares if there used to be an App for that? Google and Apple are at war and Google has also given search ranking preference to mobile enabled sites. Most Apps don't run on all types of phones and the majority offer a paltry set of features versus a website.

You also shouldn't have a separate mobile site. The duplicate content is penalized in search engines and the development costs to maintain are also double. Winners in their industry will be the first to publish responsive websites.

The mantra is often content is king and you should publish something compelling weekly. I'd argue that content is a distant third behind strategy and design. Weekly is a good metric, but monthly is more attainable especially if you focus on quality. The best posts are when you uniquely answer customer questions or greatly improve upon what is available on the web using a skyscraper analogy. Finally, approaches like expanded lists give readers bite sized content to try or research a point of interest and come back later.

Give it away. Not all your secrets, but something of value like a 21-page report of your industry. Show your expertise and besides how many people are you reaching leaving that knowledge in your head or on the file server? Competitors may try to copy you, but the source and author make them quickly exposed.

No, you shouldn't be a one trick pony. Besides a website, write a revealing book and become an authority. Then have warming events and giveaways. Supercharge your search rankings and have something noteworthy to publicize as well.

All of which leads to the concept of marketing oil wells. Smile and dial, SPAM e-mail, and dropping by in person hasn't worked for over a decade. Get smarter and have several campaigns that run continuously like events, webcasts or podcasts, and regular blog or newsletter. Identify your dream customers and target what they need so they will come to you.

Finally, measure sales and not how well you rank or how smart you seem. Last year, the published number was something like 48 times that a customer must see your name or hear your pitch before they buy. You'll have some miserable failures, but the most common mistake is trying something once or twice and then stopping. It often takes six months to a year before you can measure how viable a marketing campaign is for your business.

Does Your Website Show Customers That You're Serious About Security?

On August 6, 2014, Google announced HTTPS as a ranking signal. Essentially, encrypted websites using HTTPS would get a slight ranking boost in Google search results for being more secure and trustworthy.

The search industry exploded in pandemonium after the bulletin. The implication was that eventually only secure websites would be seen as credible. Conspiracy theorists railed that Google just wanted to start selling SSL certificates, while preventing the analysis of keywords to sell more advertising.

Moderates pointed out that there were a dozen more important tactics to improve search rankings.

Following the massive government surveillance disclosed by Edward Snowden, the debate has raged on the balance between national security and information privacy. Regardless, Google claims that it just wants to make the Internet safer. The muddy reality is encryption prevents tracking, adds cost and complexity, and the effect on information content is unknown.

Matrixforce was one of the first managed IT service providers to encrypt our website to show customers we are serious about security.

Our motivation is not better search results, but rather a commitment to security and credibility. According to Forbes, 30,000 websites are hacked each day. As reported by SINTEF in "Big Data for Better or Worse", 90% of all the data in the world has been generated online in the last two years. Unfortunately, how trustworthy is all that new data?

Here are the key things to know about implementing encryption for your website:

- **Controversial choice:** Sites like Builtwith.com show less than 20% of major websites use SSL by default. Technology juggernauts like Apple have just recently implemented SSL by default. No major news organizations have encrypted their sites. Virtually no Search Engine Optimization firms utilize HTTPS.

- **Duplicates problem:** Most sites don't redirect all traffic to HTTPS and return HTTP versions of pages giving duplicate content discredited with lower search rankings. Consult a professional for executing this strategy and updating analytics.

- **Different motivation:** SSL is about protection and will only slightly improve search results. For big search boosts, see the Search Engine Watch article "7 Things That Will Improve SEO More Than SSL". Our site traffic went up over 400% when we implemented Managed Services First Bootstrap Website with clean URLs having no extensions.

- **Greater commitment:** Your website is an intangible asset to educate and entertain customers, while providing a needed product or service. You'll spend $400 – $800 for a 4-year SSL certificate and your organization must be verifiable. If you are worried about security, then you likely put extra dedication into quality content. Understanding traffic does become more difficult, but customers readily see and appreciate your commitment versus the competition.

We feel it's more important to provide better security for customers, even if it means we lose some visibility into search analytics. If we all provided more relevant information from secure sites, the Internet would be a safer and more reputable place.

10 Modern About Page Tips

While About pages may be timeless, the fact remains that the presentation and approach will continue to change. Since the world didn't end in 2012 and you've decided to leave Vault 21, the following are the most important aspects for engaging your audience:

1. **Credibility**. If you don't have an About page, no one can verify who you are. Get in the game. Anyone who is anonymous is either clueless, scared, or doing something illicit.

2. **Authorship**. That's right. This is where you add to your author rank and place the code to get your mug next to search results.

3. **Audience**. Cue the music. Carly Simon begins "You're so vain …". It's not *about* you, but what you do for your audience. Tell them succinctly right up front.

4. **Interesting**. Now that was a pretty good blog post. Let's see who – and then you can pretty much hear the brakes screeching in your mind. The worst mistake after not having an about page is hitting your readers with 5 paragraphs of text or boring rows of author pictures with bylines.

5. **Research**. There are many great about page examples and articles on the web, but you should check out your competition too. When you all are leading and pretty much say the same stuff, you'll become a little more motivated to improve your about page.

6. **Media**. Have a pleasing layout, tell a visual story with graphics rather than text, and throw in a video or podcast. Take that 4Ws and 1H of paragraphs and transform them into something more compelling.

7. **Brevity**. It's a date. Use a unique angle and hold something back. People want an impression at a glance and won't scroll more than once.

8. **Factual**. For whatever reason, seeing numbers breaks the monotony of a sea of text while providing validity. Possibly you were the first whatever. Remember that the numbers must be defensible.

9. **Actionable**. Yes, you must have a photo, contact information, and social media icons. Woven into the mix, decide how overtly you want to make your pitch or simply ask to follow and like.

10. **Dynamic**. At least annually, update your about pages using the tips above. Think different and don't have the same boring lines for profile pages around the web either. Personalize each profile to fit the service. Now, go fix your about page.

It's Time to Get a Blog

You're struggling with what to put in all those company status updates for Facebook, Twitter, LinkedIn, and Google+. Say nothing and your organization is out of touch. Post anything just for the sake of posting like "Happy Friday!" and you're just clueless.

While the New York Times has been trying to declare blogging dead for the last 5 years, the truth is that it has just taken many different forms and is more popular than ever. So why not have a growing asset that you can inexpensively publicize and draw buyers to you? Oh, by the way, you then have your little piece of the web to promote on those social media sites, without having to struggle with what to say.

We started blogging nearly 5 years ago when a new startup began outranking our 35-year-old firm on Google. As part of an overall inbound marketing strategy, blogging has doubled our sales replacing 4 sales people for just 1% of the cost. Today, we're an up and coming blog, but our success has really been from helping clients by arming them with information to help their business.

We utilize WordPress.com for the most flexibility and the least hassle – no complicated website integration or server to maintain. Get up to speed quickly with our "25 Expert WordPress.com Principles" (blog.matrixforce.com). You can do blogging yourself and should plan on 3-5 hours each week to research, develop and publicize your posts.

Marketing firms will tell you to publish daily and better yet three times per day. It seems a little disingenuous since the more you want them to produce, the more you pay. Posting a weekly relevant article for your customers (that is not about you) will put you light years ahead of your competition.

10 Ways to Leverage Your Press Release

Marketing and advertising agencies love press releases. Included in your representation, when they write a press release for you, your approved post is syndicated online automatically. And while press releases do lots of great things for you online, like boost your profile in the search engines, there are also lots of other great things that you can do with your press releases to create even more leverage. Below is a top 10 list of suggestions.

1. Submit your press release to your local newspaper or business journal

Contact your local newspaper or business journal to find out the appropriate contact person who will be instrumental in getting your press release published and develop a friendly business relationship with that person. Find out their submission protocol and format for press releases and abide by it. Always include your name and contact information in case they have questions about your submission. Also, find out how much lead time they need to get your press releases in print, this is especially important if your press release is time sensitive. Don't forget to thank your contact person and show them appreciation periodically by taking them to lunch or sending them a small gift card to a local coffee shop. A little kindness will go a long way in building your relationship with the contact person.

2. Submit your press release to the local television and radio news sources

When submitting your press releases to local television and radio stations, take a similar approach as described under "Submit your press release to your local newspaper or business journal" above. Also take into consideration the following: Is your story of interest to a mass audience? Can it be told simply and concisely? Will it grab the attention of a consumer? Can it be done in 30 seconds or less? These are all things your radio or television station will consider so be prepared.

3. Submit your press release to the trade publications associated with your industry

The same tips apply here as are described under "Submit your press release to your local newspaper or business journal" above. Each trade publication will have their individual set of requirements. Developing an ongoing business relationship with key people within their organization cannot be stressed enough.

4. Email your press release to your clients and/or email distribution list

Your clients have a special interest in you. They will be very interested in knowing about updated news related to your professional upward movement. Utilize your email distribution list to keep your clients and prospects updated on your accomplishments. This will also serve as an opportunity to get your name in front of your clients and prospects as a reminder that you are there for them.

5. Create a direct mail card based on your press release and mail it to your direct mail distribution list

Direct mail isn't dead by any means, just ask anyone running for political office. Direct mail can be an effective means to stay in touch with your clients and prospects. By creating a good looking direct mail piece with the content of your press release, you will have another opportunity to reach your audience with important information about you and your business.

6. Create a podcast out of your press release

You can do this very easily by simply having someone read your press release into a microphone and recording it. Another variation of this would be to have someone interview you based on the information in your press release and record the interview. The recording can then be published to sites such as iTunes, Podbean or BlogTalkRadio. You can also archive your podcasts on your website so your website visitors can listen to information about your achievements. This can be an especially good resource on your mobile site.

7. Print your press release in your newsletter or blog

Many businesses have newsletters they send to their clients, customers, and/or prospects— and we certainly recommend that you should have one too! Press releases contain great information that you can use as content in your regular publication.

8. Add your press release to your website

Make sure your website has a "news" or "pulse" tab where you can begin archiving your press releases. Having an archive of press releases tells your website visitors that you are active, making news, and moving forward. Press releases support your credibility as a professional and as an expert in your business. Let your website visitors have a historical view of what you have accomplished by posting your press releases and archiving them.

9. Post your press release to your Facebook page

Most businesses have a Facebook presence. If you don't, you should. Use this form of social media to let your Facebook fans know about your most recent accomplishment by posting your press release on your Facebook page. Whenever your fans "comment" or "like" your post it has a greater likelihood of being seen by potentially hundreds of others. If they "share" your post it has the potential of being "shared" countless times by people you don't even know.

10. Tweet your press release on Twitter

Twitter is another social media tool that you can use to promote yourself and your business. You can send a message (a "tweet") on Twitter and attach a link to your press release. Twitter also makes available the potential of having others "re-tweet" your press release so that it will be seen by countless Twitter subscribers.

Chapter 15: LinkedIn Ranking and Security

10 Tips for LinkedIn Ranking

Why is your Virtual CIO telling you about LinkedIn? <u>Because LinkedIn is not the business version of Facebook to post your resume, it's a business search engine to be found.</u> That means jobs, products, services, customers, and prospects. What kind of statement does your obscurity or apathy say versus your peers or competition – much less to customers and potential prospects? And if you're thinking that all "I ever do is search for people or companies", then type something like "payroll service" (or your line of business) and watch in amazement that *people* are displayed. Then be honest about how good you are about keeping up with your contacts. LinkedIn lets you do that while your connections regularly update you too.

So now, your first reaction is to rip through the profile wizard in just a few minutes and go on to real work. Like most things in business, the most obvious approach is rarely the right one. While you congratulate yourself on a digital resume, your profile will be incredibly boring and minimally useful to anyone else. You're supposed to add some personality and reasons for others to connect with you. Write dialog for people and use keywords of how you would like to be found. The following are a few tips from my own profile:

1. **Professional "Headline" is not your job title**. From CEO at Matrixforce to Managed Services and Cloud Computing Expert – which says more about me? More importantly, it's the first place to add keywords of how I want to be found. Besides, your title is listed immediately below in Current and Past positions.

2. **You need a picture so people can actually see who you are**. Use one of how you want to be perceived for business and not the Facebook casual Saturday or funny pet picture.

3. **Website links should not say Company Website or My Blog**. You missed the boat too, if you were creative and changed the generic terms to your company name and a call to action like Read My Blog. Again, these links should be the anchor text of how you want these sites to be found in any search engine. In my case, Managed Services rather than the company name Matrixforce.

4. **Get a Twitter account**. It's another way to engage and if you're lazy like me, I link Twitter to other services so one post hits LinkedIn and any other connected services without having to go to those sites. Post something when you have something useful or relevant to say – not a micro-blog of your mundane daily activities. Give three times before you ask or sell.

5. **Personalize your Profile link** because it is more readable and shows that you really get it: http://www.linkedin.com/in/kevinfream

6. **Summary should be in first person rather than third**. It should be brief and a call to action like e-mail or call is acceptable. Try not to brag about how big or how many, but rather what is in it for the reader who hopefully was looking for your keywords. Specialties should again have a handful of keyword phrases. My previous summary was some copy from a corporate website that in retrospect seemed either arrogant or historical.

7. **Move sections around to be different and put strengths or most useful content upfront**. I moved

my blog below the summary and will likely add an upcoming video above the summary.

8. **Uh oh. Now it's time for Experience. Where is that old resume? Don't even go there**. Tell what the company does in a brief sentence. Then in first person, tell your role like a value proposition. Put a few bullets for accomplishments and (you guessed it) work in some of your keywords. Company name and title should link to those companies or people with similar titles. Don't go crazy and add spam keywords to your company name or title. It looks absurd and is a general turn off for the reader.

9. **If you haven't gotten the hint, the other part of social media is giving some information away**. So why not add some applications to show a presentation or video, listings, portfolio of offerings, publications, or events. Give something valuable to the reader, but don't give away the farm or arm competitors with anything that is not public information. For example, I automated cost comparisons and used them as landing pages for projects.

10. **You know those groups at the bottom**? Well they should have your keywords and it's great to understand your industry, but what if you participated in some customer groups?

It may take you a couple of hours to really fill out your profile completely. Note, that you should be able to raise your ranking significantly and possibly to the first page. However, unless you truly are the leader for an industry segment, you won't be able to game the system. The best way to rank highest is to provide a large amount of high quality content for people who want to connect with you.

That leads to the next topic of connecting. Some of you will stop at a complete profile taking solace in the fact that you now make a positive impression and others will start connecting, posting, and discussing. The next time you get another LinkedIn invitation and simply click accept, you better make sure your profile doesn't make you look foolish. Start getting acquainted with this business tool.

Noteworthy LinkedIn Company Updates

Are your LinkedIn Company Updates noteworthy? For many small and medium businesses, this is a tough question. Your competition is posting and so are your customers. However, are you just adding more spam to the world? Better yet, are you giving a good impression to customers and prospects?

Noteworthy – worthy of notice or attention, notable, or remarkable.

The mechanics of a good company update are fairly simple:

1. **Unique headline**
2. **Link to compelling content**
3. **Image or rich media like an infographic or video**

Google that title or blurb and you'll know if it's the same drivel that's been heard from a dozen other sources or really something unique. Generally, the link should be to a post on your blog or media site that contains an inviting featured image. Alternatively, you can post a compelling title from media on YouTube or SlideShare.

If your organization doesn't have one, then it's time to get a blog. A blog lets you answer customers questions that they need to make buying decisions. More importantly, you have a notable message and avoid some common LinkedIn Company Update mistakes:

- Happy Friday!
- Greetings from your friends
- Get to know your team
- Did you know we provide …
- There's lots going on at XYZ, Inc.
- ABC Corp is in the top list of …
- Sponsor of some event
- Have you checked out our website lately?

- Check out this product
- Just finished another ...
- Solid quarter revenue performance

All bullets above are either desperate, mundane, or outright brags. If everyone can say it or the default response is "good for you" or "so what", then you aren't posting anything interesting and it's all about you and not your customers.

It's OK to say you're hiring, have an event, new offering, or community involvement. However, great company updates tell customers how to improve their business with unique insight not found anywhere else. If you're feeling pressure, an occasional interesting industry article on a specific niche is perfectly fine.

Most organizations will want to post LinkedIn Company updates at least weekly to attract and engage followers. Look at it this way, you don't watch your favorite TV show once a month.

Consider this common scenario: a prospect is evaluating three companies on LinkedIn. One company has nothing posted, the second has some clumsy and arrogant posts, and the third offers interesting headlines with inviting images. Which company do you want to be?

Ultimate LinkedIn Security

To get the full benefits and rewards of using LinkedIn, it's important to first understand your risks and how to protect your reputation. Hundreds of millions of business professionals use LinkedIn to become more successful and be more productive. By using LinkedIn, you want to:

1. Establish a powerful personal profile.
2. Control one of the top search results for your name.
3. Keep informed about your industry.
4. Reach others that can help you.

The problem is that many LinkedIn members are unaware of privacy issues or common security settings. Annually an estimated 10% of Linked profiles are hacked, defaced, and utilized for illicit spam. This Ultimate LinkedIn Security Guide has been created to provide concise and comprehensive security usage for LinkedIn.

Understand LinkedIn Terms of Service

LinkedIn prides itself on being a "members first" company. In the past, the User Agreement and Privacy Policy gave LinkedIn broad rights to use member posted content. Although those rights were rarely exercised, LinkedIn has now narrowed content rights to specifically state that members own the content they post:

- You own your content that you post on our services.
- If you delete anything from our services, our rights to it will end.
- We don't have exclusive rights to your content.
- We don't license or sell your content to third-parties (like advertisers, publishers, and websites) without your express written permission.
- We won't alter the intent of your content.

Obviously, LinkedIn can't control what others do with your content. Some content may need to be translated or adjusted for formatting and technical reasons. Know that any posted content such as Pulse Articles are building more search authority for LinkedIn, rather than your own website or blog. That's the tradeoff for potentially more viewers (even though you own the content), but any links from LinkedIn are "nofollow" with no benefit for your site or blog in search results.

Top 5 Ways to Protect Your LinkedIn Account

LinkedIn takes member safety and privacy very seriously. By default, all LinkedIn accounts are already protected by a series of automatic checks that are designed to thwart unauthorized sign-in attempts and keep your data safe. However, there are few additional steps you can take to protect your privacy and control your digital footprint on LinkedIn.

1. Update your Privacy Settings to Disable Activity Broadcasts and Connection Views

Any time you change your profile, whatever you change is broadcast to all of your existing connections. Whenever another member visits your profile, they can see all of your connections. Likewise, when you view another member's profile, they are notified with your name, photo, and headline.

Take a look at your LinkedIn settings today to eliminate unwanted sharing:

- **Turn on/off your activity broadcasts:** Uncheck this option so your connections don't see when you make changes to your profile, follow companies, or recommend connections.

- **Select what others can see when you've viewed their profile:** Select complete privacy mode to view member information anonymously.

- **Select who can see your connections:** Thwart snooping competitors by making your connections only be visible to you.

- **Show/Hide "Viewers of this profile also viewed" box on my Profile page:** Disable this option so the focus is solely on your profile.

Note, that you can also block another member from viewing your profile or status updates. Go to the profile of the person you want to block and select "Block or Report" from the drop-down menu at the top of the profile summary.

2. Opt into Two-Step Verification to Protect Your Account from Being Hacked

LinkedIn offers members the ability to turn on two-step verification for their accounts, which will require an account password and a numeric code sent to your phone via text message whenever we don't recognize the new device you're attempting to sign in from. See the SlideShare presentation below and check out the tips on troubleshooting two-step authentication.

3. Opt into Secure Browsing (HTTPS) for Extra Protection Against Unauthorized Access to Your Activity on LinkedIn

A good indicator of a protected connection on a website starts with https://. While LinkedIn automatically secures a connection when you are on certain pages that require sensitive information (such as using a credit card), you also have the option to turn on this protected connection when viewing all pages across LinkedIn.

Learn more about turning this feature on in your account. LinkedIn is currently working on making this a default setting.

4. Change Your Password Regularly to Help Safeguard Your LinkedIn Account

Never give your password to others or write it down. While opting into two-step authentication mitigates many password vulnerabilities, always sign out of your account after you use LinkedIn. Here are some more best practices:

- Change your password every few months
- Don't use the same password on all the sites you visit
- Don't use a word from the dictionary
- Think of a meaningful phrase, song or quote and turn it into a complex password using the first letter of each word
- Randomly add capital letters, punctuation or symbols
- Substitute numbers for letters that look similar (for example, substitute "0" for "o" or "3" for "E"

5. Watch Out for Phishing Emails Requesting Personal or Sensitive Information

LinkedIn will never ask for your sensitive personal or financial information via email. To confirm whether a message is really from LinkedIn or not, here are a few things you can look for:

- All valid LinkedIn messages will contain a security footer and it's not a good practice to open any attachments or click any links in an email that seems suspicious or from an unknown party.

- Here are some indicators which should raise your suspicions that the email claiming to be from LinkedIn is **not** legitimate:

  - The message is telling you to open an email attachment or install a software update.

  - The message contains bad spelling and grammar.

  - The message contains a threat of some kind. Example: your account will be deleted unless you act right away.

Before clicking on any links within an email, it's a good idea to move your cursor over the links to see where they're directing you. In the case of an email from LinkedIn, if it's not directing you back to the LinkedIn website, you can treat the message as a phishing attempt. Visit the LinkedIn Safety Center for more information and keep up with new LinkedIn features at the Official LinkedIn Blog (http://blog.linkedin.com/).

Chapter 16: Glimpse the Modern Network and Disaster Recovery

Modern disaster recovery looks nothing like the daunting 300-page manuals of just a few years ago. Old disaster recovery plans invoke images of stacks of cash and complexity like playing the game Jenga blind. Unfortunately, the reality is most organizations don't have a disaster response plan. There is no budget for the worst-case scenario, more pressing business issues are always pushed to the forefront, and two weeks is generally the estimated delivery of replacement equipment and restoration. Few organizations face the realization that:

1. Often just one month of lost revenue likely means bankruptcy

2. Disaster recovery implementation can be done in steps

Now we're going to reveal an industry secret of how we run our business for vendor due diligence compliance for our bank, healthcare, accounting, and legal customers. This is also the same process we use to help customers achieve modern disaster recovery for half the cost and complexity of legacy alternatives (like duplicating the cost and maintenance of everything at a remote location).

First, we moved our websites externally to Network Solutions. The following year email, messaging, and all corporate data was moved to Office 365. Subsequently, we established an Azure subscription and enabled AD Connect for single password access to our network and the cloud. This year, we implemented RemoteApp for accounting and a virtual domain controller at Microsoft.

For any type of disaster, our staff can securely access systems anywhere there is Internet access. Systems are protected by Federal Information Security compliance and security audits. If the corporate facilities are destroyed, staff assist customers as normal. The only failover is switching our customer's online backup to replicated storage.

Management and administrative personnel just have the additional burdens of purchasing new facilities, equipment, furniture, and office supplies. With the new facilities operational, a site to site VPN to Microsoft Azure is established and new workstations and servers are deployed. Unlike traditional disaster recovery plans, recovery is not dependent upon the specialized knowledge of a few individuals, there is no complicated restore, and vendors may assist in accessing systems as necessary. Most importantly, customers are not impacted and revenues continue to flow.

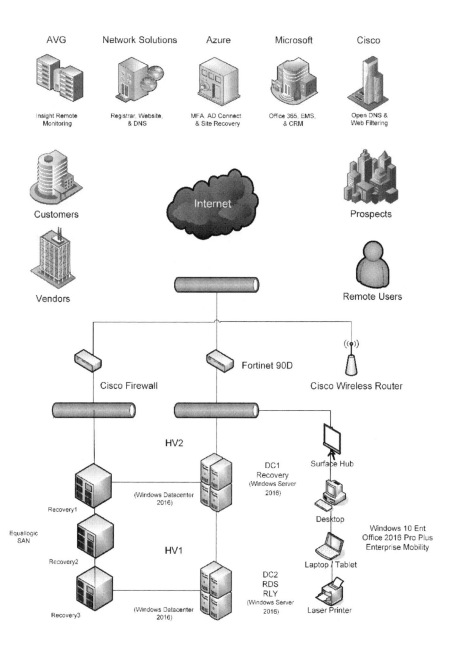

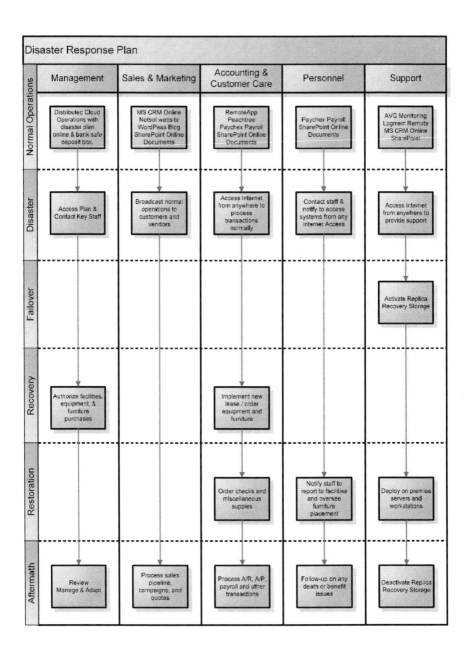

Understanding Azure Site Recovery

Azure Site Recovery provides offline copies of your virtual servers replicated to Microsoft every 15 minutes. Since 2008, the technology has existed to replicate virtual servers from a physical network across the Internet to another facility a few miles or many hours away. While disaster recovery became somewhat easier to implement, there were still four major problems:

1. Duplication of hardware costs and software licensing.

2. Significant monthly fees for disaster recovery facilities and Internet bandwidth.

3. Maintenance and monitoring of disaster recovery systems are often lacking or non-existent.

4. Failover testing to the disaster recovery site and back to headquarters was time-consuming and costly.

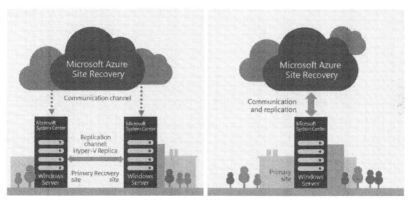

Source: Microsoft

In the event of a real disaster, you also must ask:

Would the staff leave their families or able to event get to the disaster recovery site safely?

What happens if the disaster recovery site is also destroyed and where is our data/system then replicated?

How would we recover if the Information Technology people didn't survive or weren't available?

Azure Site Recovery is just one component of our Orbit® Cloud Computing services. By leveraging Microsoft hyper-scale infrastructure and security with our Delta® methodology, we've changed the approach to modern disaster recovery. Anywhere people can access the Internet, they can securely access systems without risking their lives getting to a facility that may not be functional. For nominal cost, data is replicated to another datacenter in a different region or around the globe. If we aren't available, processes are documented with customer's having co-administrator access and the added ability to call on Microsoft directly.

Here is how site recovery works:

- **Site-to-site Virtual Private Network:** You must use a router or firewall capable of supporting Dynamic Domain Name Services (DDNS) and establish a secure connection to Microsoft.

- **Cloud configuration:** A remote network, storage, and recovery groups of servers to start in a logical order are setup and documented. Once enabled on required Windows Server 2012 R2, the first replication of servers is the longest but only small and quick incremental changes are necessary from that point forward.

- **Failover sandbox:** One of the best features is the ability to bring replicated servers online for testing without affecting your production environment. During testing, customers do incur a flat cost per machine for runtime. However, afterwards the failover machines are simply shutdown and the monthly cost returns to a nominal amount per replicated offline server.

- **Disaster failover:** In a true emergency, an actual failover of servers is brought online and accessed through pre-defined Remote Desktop Connection. Following a disaster with reconstruction of the facility and new equipment, a VPN may be reestablished to headquarters and the cloud environment replicated on-site.

Many customers struggle with simply purchasing Azure, much less documenting and retaining a staff trained in the multi-disciplines depicted above. Use this business advisory to arm yourself with questions to ask and problems to avoid when considering disaster recovery.

Chapter 17: Winning with a Hybrid Approach to Cloud Computing & Security

Unknown to most of the world, history is being made again and customers are winning big. On July 9th – 13th, 2017 in Washington DC, Matrixforce joins an elite group of Microsoft's Top 100 Cloud Champions at Microsoft Inspire. What got us here is streamlining technology for customers like you.

Disaster Recovery Failure. Before it was called cloud, we were leveraging 20 years of Microsoft competency. Then 2008 came with the worst ice storm that had ever hit Oklahoma. With as much as six inches of ice blanketing the state, many customers had no power for days. Hundreds of people died.

Traditional data centers were inundated. Many customers couldn't physically get there, much less stomach the liability of employees possibly dying to come to work. Even if you got on site and there were hosting staff to help you, you still had the problem of maintaining and replacing the equipment over time. Plus, who were these guys who now had full access to all of my data? When are they going to grow to better handle the next disaster? Where is my data replicated and now what do I do when this data center is possibly destroyed or inaccessible?

Innovation from tragedy. In 2009, Oklahoma was again hit with another ice apocalypse. This time we were ready. With Office 365, customers just had to access the Internet from anywhere to respond to e-mail and access files. There was no expensive failover or dangerous travel and new customers could be up and running in just a few hours. No other traditional rack space host can compete with the billions invested by Microsoft in unparalleled productivity and security. While the competition was celebrating by selling a bunch of planned obsolescence hardware with an avalanche of software and services, we helped customers move business forward and work smarter in the future.

Continual Vigilance. It's called eating your own dog food which means we run our business on Azure, Office 365, Intune, and CRM Online. We've already made all the mistakes deploying and continually learning, as an example for customers and our commitment to expertise. We share specialized operational knowledge, rather than scripted marketing hype. Always make a technology provider prove their worth by having them demonstrate cloud in their business.

Fearmongering. The stark reality is that only about 5% of the 640,000 Microsoft Partners worldwide conduct business on cloud. They push fear because a traditional partner is losing 70% of their revenue versus offering cloud. We challenge you to search the web for a story on Office 365 getting hacked. All of those cautionary tales pertain to consumer offerings with obviously limited focus on security. Once customers actually do their own investigation, they are pleasantly surprised about the Office 365 Comparison savings for built-in disaster recovery, backup, security, and productivity.

Cloud Commitment. This is the 15th annual Microsoft Inspire (formerly Worldwide Partner Conference) and we now have nearly 10 years of experience moving Oklahoma and national customers to the cloud. Our new goal is 100,000 subscribers. Unlike the CRN 250 or Inc 5000 list, Microsoft Top 100 Cloud Champion is not purchased advertising. Our customers enjoy huge savings and new capabilities as competitive advantage versus a Dell Partner of the Year that simply means a reseller sold a bunch of equipment. Any provider who has not started providing cloud services with at least 5,000 subscribers, is a high-risk choice for your business without enough revenue to survive or competency to deliver.

Customer Champions. Cloud Champion attendees will be provided advanced notice and exclusive training under Non-

Disclosure Agreement on Microsoft Azure, Windows 10, Partner Center, and Vision. Further, structured break-out sessions are tailored per partner focus to provide unparalleled skills for customers.

Following this leading-edge training, Matrixforce will begin providing even more breakthrough services for better productivity in the cloud and briefing managed services clients on strategic approach.

Hybrid Office 365 Cloud Comparison

Here's a common scenario of a 50-employee business with an aging e-mail server and dated copies of Microsoft Office. Unlike Google, customers using Microsoft Online Services can pick and choose the applications and data they put in the cloud and use local applications independent of Internet availability.

This hybrid approach means customers can leverage high security and disaster recovery at a fraction of build-your-own or rented brick-and-mortar disaster recovery facilities, while enjoying productivity and privacy options they prefer.

Hybrid Cloud Value Proposition Comparison

Cost	2017	2018	2019	2020	2021	Total
On-Premise Exchange (50 users)						
Server Hardware (2)	18,400			18,400		$36,800
Windows Server 2016 Datacenter (2)	12,478			12,478		$24,956
Exchange Server Enterprise 2016 (2)	6,128			6,128		$12,256
Exchange Client Access	9,000			9,000		$18,000
Microsoft Office	39,950			39,950		$79,900
SSL Certificate	889			889		$1,778
Upgrade Project	9,254			9,254		$18,508
Webfiltering / Cybersecurity	3,279	3,279	3,279	3,279	3,279	$16,395
System Monitoring / Security Updates	2,953	2,953	2,953	2,953	2,953	$14,765
Anti-Virus and Anti-malware	2,488	2,488	2,488	2,488	2,488	$12,440
Anti-Spam / Encrypted E-mail	6,057	6,057	6,057	6,057	6,057	$30,285
Backup Sofware/Hardware	17,352	17,352	17,352	17,352	17,352	$86,760
Legacy Replacement	**128,228**	**32,129**	**32,129**	**128,228**	**32,129**	**$352,843**
Office 365 (50 Users)						
Upgrade Project	6,879					$6,879
Office 365 E3 $20/Mo/User	12,000	12,000	12,000	12,000	12,000	$60,000
Online Backup Email/OneDrive	4,800	4,800	4,800	4,800	4,800	$24,000
Overwatch EMS/Cyber/Compliance	11,950	11,950	11,950	11,950	11,950	$59,750
New Technology	**35,629**	**28,750**	**28,750**	**28,750**	**28,750**	**$150,629**
Savings	**92,599**	**3,379**	**3,379**	**99,478**	**3,379**	**202,214**
%	**72%**	**11%**	**11%**	**78%**	**11%**	**57%**

Features		New		Legacy		
Digital Offsite Backup		Yes		No		
Global Geo-Dispersed Data Centers		Yes		No		
Cybertrust Certification		Yes		No		
Save on Projects		Yes		No		
Easy Upgrades		Yes		No		

Legacy on-premise solutions have striking peaks and valleys for cost. Often forgotten is the fact that two each of critical servers and related software is required for best uptime and disaster recovery. The waterfall effect of new software also demands updated applications, security, and backup. Businesses are really upside down on cost when you consider that services like Office 365 cover 5 devices per user for less than traditional options.

Same Sign-on Explained

To save confusion and increase productivity, many customers want the same password for local networks and the cloud. "ADConnect" is a Microsoft Azure Active Directory Sync tool that synchronizes user passwords from your on-premises Active Directory to Azure Active Directory ("Azure AD"). This feature enables your users to log into their Azure Active Directory services (such as Office 365, Intune, CRM Online, etc.) using the same password as they use to log into your on-premises network. It is important to note that this feature does not provide a Single Sign-On (SSO) solution.

For existing on-premises infrastructure, the Azure ADConnect tool is deployed on one domain controller. Then Azure Active Directory is simply linked to the local Active Directory and synchronization verified. When synchronizing passwords using the password sync feature, the plain text version of a user's password is neither exposed to the password sync tool nor to Azure AD or any of the associated services. Additionally, there is no requirement on the on-premises Active Directory to store the password in a reversibly encrypted format. When you enable password sync, the password complexity policies configured in the on-premises Active Directory override any complexity policies that may be defined in the cloud for synchronized users.

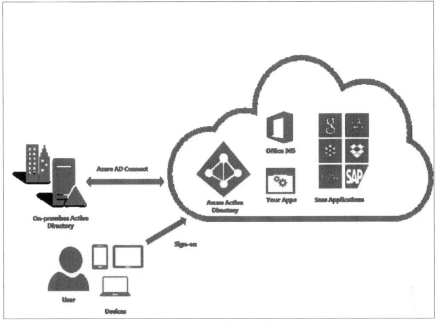

Source: Microsoft

Deploying Azure Active Directory synchronization is the recommended scenario for customers wishing to have the same password in the cloud and on the network. Unlike 6 servers required for true SSO, this approach requires no integration of VPN or virtual machine components at Microsoft Azure. When Microsoft fully implements Active Directory Premium, customers may deploy single sign-on for Active Directory and third-party services without virtual machines for less than Starbucks for $6 per user per month.

ADConnect allows you to effectively support any Microsoft Online Services with the same local password hash, without complex infrastructure integration. Azure Single Sign-On or Active Directory Premium may always be added in the future. With this scenario, the customer avoids a site to site VPN and can access both the local directory and Microsoft Online Services if directory synchronization is interrupted.

Office 365 Backup Recommendations

Office 365 offers unprecedented disaster recovery and security compliance, but you must enable features to replace traditional backup and take practical precautions.

Ignorance is not bliss. If you want to strike fear into the heart of any system administrator, tell them they must do disaster recovery of the Exchange or SharePoint servers. Better yet, just tell them you need a folder or two from both systems for a couple of users from 6 months ago. Most administrators don't have the firsthand knowledge of the steps required or real-life experience of recovering from a disaster. Then there are all the unknowns: power, Internet, facilities, available hardware, software media, recorded settings, free disk space, and valid backup.

Horribly broken model. Whether you recognize it or not, the two scenarios above are vastly different for data protection and restoration. The whole reason you're considering Office 365 is availability, security, and productivity. Your backup is always broken or assumed to be functioning. Data is perpetually growing and systems are aging, but it's nearly impossible to get budget for upgrades. A single individual or tiny group of overworked and highly stressed IT professionals are then supposed to keep up with the latest technology, regulations, and system issues – day or night, as well as weekends and holidays.

Moving the monkey. The old monolithic model is costly and fraught with risk. Microsoft offers over 19 regions of data centers for data replication with the world's leading security and privacy. So, the first scenario of disaster recovery is covered. Anywhere you can reach the Internet, you have your documents and e-mail on a smartphone to a traditional PC. Without the Internet, you have a copy of your mailbox the last time you connected and whatever documents you have downloaded or synched with your OneDrive.

What most people think of as backup is not provided by Office 365, because compliance features offer faster recovery.

Manage business exceptions. If the statement above scares you, it shouldn't because there are multiple levels of data protection with Office 365. What everyone has to consider is how often do you have to restore past 30 days and what is your true data policy? Unfortunately, few customers understand or take advantage data protection settings:

- **Exchange:** Local mailbox copy on every synched device, recover deleted items, online archive, retention policy, journaling, legal hold, encryption, and data loss prevention rules.

- **SharePoint:** Synchronized documents on OneDrive and any SharePoint sites, previous versions, and user/admin/site recycle bin.

Avoid common mistakes. After an e-mail or data migration to Office 365, customers are happy not to be shackled by previous system limitations and appreciate ready access to data from virtually anywhere. However, many data protection settings are not enabled by default:

1. Recover deleted items should be increased from 14 to 30 days.

2. Online archives must also be enabled using a PowerShell archive cmdlet for all users.

3. A separate user mailbox must be purchased of Exchange Plan 2 or higher with a journaling mail flow rule to blind carbon copy every message sent and received, along with a custom journal retention policy to move messages to the associated online archive monthly to quarterly.

4. A defined records retention policy is strongly recommended to manage the quantity of mail and more importantly limit legal risk to the organization.

5. Litigation hold may be enabled on or before litigation for both e-mail and documents.

6. Previous versions of files are enabled by default for OneDrive, but must be enabled for all other SharePoint sites.

Take practical precautions. Once you have verified or corrected any of the common mistakes, you can focus on higher business continuity concepts. E-mail journaling, retention archiving (consult an attorney), and litigation hold negate numerous versions of backup. You are well protected with Office 365 for e-mail and document availability, security, disaster recovery, and archiving. However, those features must be monitored on a regular basis and Office 365 has no external backup options. To not have all your eggs in one basket, some customers are choosing third-party online backup services for both Office 365 Exchange and SharePoint.

Chapter 18: Questions You Should Your Current IT Consultant

Trust and Security:

Q1: **What type of legal entity is their organization?**

Our Answer: Matrixforce is an Oklahoma C Corporation, originally established in 1978. Unlike a Limited Liability Company (LLC), the ownership and nature of business are clearly listed by the Secretary of State. When trust is paramount, you don't want to unknowingly expose your proprietary information to foreign entities, illicit businesses, felons, absentee owners, or competitors. Likewise, there is no regulating board for the technology industry. "Consulting" firms that are not actually Professional Service Corporations are misleading and regularly targeted by federal authorities for legal and tax fraud.

Q2: **How are technical and sales staff compensated and how is performance measured?**

Our Answer: Employees are paid salary, plus profit-sharing bonus. No one is compensated by billable hours or sales of product. Performance is measured by customer satisfaction and communication with required goals for system plan updates, case follow-up, standard operating procedures, and informational articles and videos. Our employees are only motivated to help your business.

Q3: **How do they maintain confidentiality and utilize solutions internally?**

Our Answer: All staff are full time employees and U.S. citizens who sign an employment agreement requiring confidentiality and consenting to an annual background check. We run our business on the same solutions we support to streamline our technology too. Amazingly, many providers don't utilize their own products and services to understand usage or gain internal benefits. Plus, utilizing contract labor or individuals with poor credit or legal problems puts customers at high risk.

Q4: What is their specialty and how will it help your business?

Our Answer: Managed services is our only business, focusing strictly on midsized organizations in professional services, financial, industry, and public sectors. We streamline your technology to reduce complexity, improve operations, and lower costs. The disingenuous platitude "Let us manage your technology, so you can focus on business" has little business benefit, except possibly convenience. However, when can you ignore any part of your business, much less abdicate control of vital proprietary data? Hardware and software resellers survive by selling more product from partners, while recruiting firms want to regularly replace an employee.

Q5: Where is their cloud and does it adhere to the Federal Information Security Act?

Our Answer: We utilize Microsoft Azure with 19 regions of geo-dispersed data centers offering the world's largest hyper-scale capacity of storage and compute power, along with FISMA compliance. Unburdened by maintaining data center facilities or complicated failover, we specialize in processes to improve operations and keep your business running.

Local or regional providers struggle with maintaining facilities and only meet basic security regulations. White label or rebranding of local data center services by small providers also raises concerns about questionable ownership and competency, while still not complying with the highest security standards.

Customer Service:

Q6: **Are they serious about availability, like providing individual cell phone and alternate numbers?**

Our Answer: We provide customers the cell numbers of their support team, as well as our own management. In addition, we publish an emergency number for non-business hours, weekends, holidays, and during emergent situations such as inclement weather. It's incredibly frustrating to have network issues and not be able to contact support for help.

Q7: **Do they have a written guaranteed response time for support?**

Our Answer: When you enter a case through the customer portal or send an e-mail to support@matrixforce.com, you get an immediate notification and a support specialist is assigned. Most cases are resolved within the hour using remote assistance tools. Most service providers don't have any guaranteed response time. However, we offer a standard 2 or 4 hour guaranteed response as part of our Guardian Managed Services agreement.

Q8: **Do they have a methodology to explain what they are doing and answer your questions in simple terms without being arrogant or making you feel stupid?**

Our Answer: Our support staff receive annual training in rules of engagement and customer service as part of our patent pending Delta methodology: explain and document upfront, regularly communicate status, and follow-up afterward. Much like a bedside manner for doctors, support specialists learn approach and examples of appropriate and inappropriate responses to customer questions.

Q9: **Do they offer degreed and certified management team to help you implement your technology strategy on a quarterly basis?**

Our Answer: Our management team conducts quarterly meetings with our clients to review: 5-year plan, system overview and status, strategy scorecard, problem areas with recommendations, and industry technology updates. The goal with these meetings is helping clients be more profitable, efficient, and competitive. Our leadership each have 4-year degrees and 20+ years of experience and certification. You wouldn't trust your life to a doctor who wasn't licensed, so why would you trust your business to a technology advisor without a degree?

Q10: **Do they submit a case description and resolution with follow-up on each issue?**

Our Answer: We provide an automated case description with resolution when the case is closed and the assigned support specialist contacts the user to answer any other questions afterwards. These same cases are available on-demand and typed by category to review problem areas.

Q11: Do they assume the risk and provide flat cost projects?

Our Answer: All projects are fixed-priced, so we assume the risk for any mitigating circumstances and are motivated to finish in a timely manner. This is important because many service providers only quote "time and materials," which gives them free rein to nickel-and-dime you as well as take as much time as they want on completing a project.

System Assurance:

Q12: Do they insist on remotely monitoring your network 24x7 and ensure devices are up-to-date for anti-malware and security updates whether local or remote?

Our Answer: Yes, our Insight® remote monitoring watches over your network to constantly alert us for developing problems before they become bigger issues. Unique cloud device management enforces device security settings wherever a connection is made to the Internet. Support specialists have the capability to provide remote assistance or restart devices, as well as lock or wipe a device in case of loss or theft.

Q13: Do they provide self-service reporting of system status and health of the network?

Our Answer: On demand, our clients may access a secure dashboard to get a detailed report that shows an overall health score of their network and specific hardware and software information of each device.

Q14: Is it standard procedure to provide written network documentation detailing critical

information or are they the only person with the "keys to the kingdom"?

Our Answer: All clients receive a System Plan in written and electronic form at no additional cost that includes: critical contact information, passwords, license keys and important system tags, overview diagram, naming conventions, application settings, and security policies. System plans are updated before each project and separate Standard Operating Procedures like workstation setup are also provided.

Q15: **Do they have more than one technician that is familiar with your network in case they leave the company, get sick, or go on vacation?**

Our Answer: Yes, we assign a team of 5 support specialists that all utilize the System Plan, Case Management, Insight Monitoring, and Standard Operating Procedures. Clients get a high level of support and are not impacted by personnel changes or temporary absences.

Q16: **Do they INSIST on monitoring online backup or are they letting you rely on outdated tape technology or external hard drives?**

Our Answer: We do not allow our clients to use tape backups because they are incredibly unreliable. External drives don't get a copy of the data out of the building and are prone to shorts and disk errors. We make sure all of our clients have encrypted online backup at 1.5x to 6x compression and retention for 30 days, 12 months, and 3 years.

Q17: **Do they perform a weekly manual analysis of systems or just mindlessly accept automated alerts?**

Our Answer: Weekly we do an eyes-on review of systems to check for anomalies the monitoring may not catch and analyze trends, rather than just responding to alerts. While the monitoring technology is very reliable, testing is a fatal flaw for the industry and just another example of our commitment and diligence.

Q18: Is their help desk US-based or outsourced to an overseas company or third party?

Our Answer: We provide our own in-house help desk using English speaking Americans that are trained to be friendly and knowledgeable. We consider this differentiator one of the most important aspects of customer service, plus we feel it's important for keeping your data secure.

Q19: Is the initial technician answering the phone capable of resolving the issue or must you transfer to three other levels?

Our Answer: We cross-train so you get a support specialist capable of answering your questions, performing remote support, and resolving the issue. Our specialists own the problem and use best practice cut-off points for intervening with the manufacturer. The legacy approach of a case coordinator who transfers you through 4 levels of help desk support is frustrating, time consuming, and ineffectual.

Q20: Do their technicians maintain current vendor certifications and publish knowledgebase articles, blog posts, and videos – or are they learning on your dime and not transferring knowledge?

Our Answer: Matrixforce is the exclusive Microsoft Gold Cloud Solution Partner for Oklahoma where our support specialists maintain annual certification and support over 150 customers and 25,000 subscribers annually with third-party audited 97% satisfaction rating. For thought leadership and self-service education, we have published weekly blog posts, knowledge base articles, and videos for over a decade.

Q21: What kind of plan do they offer and what are the "gotchas"?

Our Answer: Our Guardian® Managed Services are flat cost for unlimited incidents and regular monitoring and system assurance. Guardian® is a flexible offering based upon the number of servers and users supported. The only time you pay additional cost is when you purchase products or have a flat cost project, such as implementing a new server.

Many providers offer a choice of various support options ending with the "all-inclusive" plan. While the other plans seem limited, it's an obvious warning sign that the all-inclusive plan is listed last likely meaning rarely sold or lacking confidence or experience in delivery. However, make sure you really understand what is and is not included. Some things to consider are:

- Is there a no obligation probationary period?
- Are services flat cost, hourly blocks of time, or some combination?
- What tasks or items specifically are NOT included?
- Is hardware and/or software included?
- What about 3rd-party software support?
- Is there non-performance cancellation at no additional cost?

- Is online backup included and to what degree?
- What is the cost of growth in additional users or servers?
- What about on-site support calls? Or support to remote users?

Chapter 19: Scary Facts About IT Firms

Few Technology Firm Owners Are Competent

You absolutely would not risk your health, reputation, or money going to people who were not professional doctors, lawyers, and accountants. However, many organizations regularly gamble with information technology that could lead to life threatening stress, costly litigation, and bankruptcy.

Unlike other professional services, information technology is not tied to an institution like insurance, courts, or government. There is little formal education required and no ongoing learning that is mandatory with other professions via Continuing Professional Education (CPE). While virtually every technology firm touts "certified" on their website, what does that really mean? The fact remains few technology firm owners are competent.

Often the main person you depend upon for implementing and supporting technology for your business has limited education and no verified learning since. Ask the owner of your IT services firm these two questions:

1) What is your degree, where was it from, and what year?

2) When and what was your last CPE?

You'll be astonished to find most owners don't have a 4-year degree in technology or business. Also, the online webinar last week about some manufacturer's latest product doesn't count as skills growth or learning. Some people may argue that technology owners shouldn't be required to keep current because it's not their role. Nonetheless, the technology billionaires who achieved their success without a degree can be counted on one hand. In an industry that is now updating products and services every three months, how can anyone responsibly advise customers without annual training?

In 1989, I graduated with a Bachelor of Science degree in Management Information Systems from the University of Tulsa. That might as well have been a lifetime ago in technology and a few subscriptions to trade rags would not have made an accomplished authority today. Since 1994, I have had a specialization as a Microsoft Certified IT Professional. Recently, 70-347 Enabling Office 365 Services was added to my transcript for a firm accreditation held by no other state provider.

While I don't provide mainline support, customers appreciate dealing with an expert that can demonstrate and help evaluate vital technology for their business. They also recognize a well-rounded business leader growing a firm 20% per year that can offer business insights for them as well.

Fortunately for customers, the technology industry has broadened forcing service providers to focus on a niche, as no firm can "do it all" any longer. Some of my peers have comparable or better qualifications, but the vast majority of competitors are led by lacking and irrelevant skills of a past era. **Customers should know that certifications like Microsoft Certified System Engineer are no longer valid.**

While this revelation be controversial and seen as bashing the competition, it's unknowing customers that are most at risk. Many online backup customers come to us following a data loss, just like managed IT services and cloud computing customers come to us after security breaches or significant downtime. Even if you're happy with your current provider, you should ask the two questions above. If you don't like the answer, start looking for a better alternative.

10 Things to Know About Microsoft Partners

With over 20 years of experience as a Microsoft Partner, clients and peers often don't realize what the designation means:

1. **Everyone is a Microsoft Partner**. That is an exaggeration, but there are over 640,000 Microsoft Partners worldwide.

2. **Microsoft is a good partner**. For about $2,000 per year, Partners get tens of thousands of dollars in software and services.

3. **Microsoft recognizes sales**. Only partners that do a very high volume of sales of Microsoft products and services get extra recognition and support from Microsoft.

4. **There are many flavors**. Some partners sell hardware and software, many develop apps, most offer services, and lots of partners do a combination of these things.

5. **Margins are slim**. Multiple levels of competition mean most partners are lucky to make even 6% on Microsoft products and services.

6. **70% are not profitable**. It's high risk for technologists and customers should pick well established players.

7. **Good partners specialize**. Technology is a broader field than legal, medical, and financial industries combined. Experts are paid for skill in specific offerings or industries and customers can readily spot them.

8. **Bad partners do everything**. It's just not possible to sell, implement, and support most facets of technology. To make ends meet and just to survive,

many Microsoft partners try to do it all. These type of partner organizations go broke, burn out employees, and damage customers.

9. **Competency rules**. There are just a couple hundred top-tier Cloud Accelerate Partners that have the experience and proven track record of moving over 2,000 subscribers per year to Microsoft Online Services. Proven knowledge and experience competency programs are replacing old Gold and Silver programs, which were just about passing tests. Most Microsoft Partner owners have little formal education and no current Microsoft certifications.

10. **Partner Center transparency**. The best partners are actually listed at Microsoft Partner Center (https://partnercenter.microsoft.com). The "me too" partners usually have just a lonely link to some sales page on their website. The experts provide full information for evaluation:

- Demo or trial
- Buy online options
- Screen shots and videos
- Additional Info
- Support and Training
- Whitepapers
- Setup and Deployment
- Specs and Reference
- Sample Code

You're Asking the Wrong Questions

I can quickly tell when a prospect is serious and a good fit. You judge by the questions. It's tough for customers as most potential vendors they see have no differentiating sales or marketing process. The message is usually a punch in the nose brag of: we are the leading whatever, do lots of great things, are overly qualified, and loved by just about everybody.

Seasoned buyers either ignore the noise or change gears to their agenda. The rub is that most customers commit nearly the same sin by asking a few standard questions that have very little relevance:

1. **How long have you been in business?** You're not really going to pick a solution by how long each company has been in business. New startups are often selected on the gamble the low cost returns a successful outcome.

2. **How many employees do you have?** Many organizations have used a single individual for multiple years or are averse to both sole proprietorships and huge corporations.

3. **How many customers do you have?** Until recently, Twitter had 15 employees with tens of millions of users making this question non-sense.

Maybe in the 80's or 90's, these questions put vendors on notice. Today, you can answer these questions in seconds on the web and they don't have much meaning in your selection. Trade the questions above for these:

1. **How would you solve my problem?** Move on when you get brain-lock and a "I'll get back to you on that" or an unintelligible ramble.

2. **Can you show me how you use your solution internally?** Astoundingly, most technology providers either can't afford or don't believe in the offering they are pushing. Run away if this is the case.

3. **What range of cost is usually expected upfront and going forward?** If you've done your homework, you may already have a sense of cost or found a calculator on the vendor's website. Obviously, it is inappropriate to start with cost, but a vendor who doesn't know normal transaction costs knows their business less than they know yours.

It's great to follow common conventions, but everyone appreciates quickly qualifying the best customer and vendor fit.

Chapter 20: No Contract or Disruptive 1 Year Contracts

No Commitment and Hand Over Your Data

No contract, no commitment is a business reality that means if there is no agreement then you should **expect nothing – except that your data may be stolen too**. You read that right and let it sink in. We often forget this important adage and clever marketing sometimes nabs the unsuspecting, who quickly learn no obligation literally implies that you can't really complain about lousy or no service.

Think about it. What kind of IT support are you paying for like a guaranteed 4-hour response or monthly maintenance or quarterly security assessment? How about some disaster recovery documentation or self-service access to monitoring systems, so you can see your system health and whether it is being updated yourself? Really, what's included and what isn't?

You're not having your lawn mowed, you're handing your livelihood and critical files over to often unknown individuals for IT support. You already know big players like Google use your data and Internet usage for advertising, but what weasel words are on the terms page of that copier shop or sole proprietor website or invoice? Without a minimum Reciprocal Non-Disclosure Agreement or RNDA, what protection do you have for company secrets spilled to competitors or margins leaked to customers? **Beware of no contract, no commitment scams to bilk you out of money and sell your data to damage your company's reputation.**

Disruptive 1 Year Contracts

I haven't found that guy yet. He must be a slick Jerry Maguire type. Instead, maybe it's a woman like the oracle character from the Matrix, who just "knows" what is going to happen.

Regardless, I'm dying to speak with this person and find out how they perpetuated the **fraudulent idea that one-year contracts are preferred**. Try to find a text-book that teaches one-year contracts are better, or spend a few minutes on your favorite search engine. It's simply not there.

When I consistently hear "We only do one-year contracts", I just shake my head. Your office lease is 5 years or the mortgage on your building is at least 15 years. The note on the company vehicle is probably 4 years. Even your cell plan is 2 years. So, the reality is that almost nothing you do is a one-year contract.

Ask a simple question like "Do you have a 5-year plan?" and you start to uncover startling things like no budgeting and record keeping just for the sake of paying taxes. Alternatively, you have the opposite extreme where the last quarter of every year is spent scrutinizing expenses, rather than getting new business. Here's the revelation about one-year contracts:

1. **One-year contracts are disruptive.** By the time you get a contract made, you've got just 8 months before you start evaluating vendors and options for the next. Yearly transitions to new products or services are time-consuming and painful to business. For example, try moving offices each year.

2. **One-year contracts are expensive.** Vendors don't blink when you just want a one-year contract because they know their margins are better than discounted multi-year contracts, and most businesses rarely review and often just automatically renew each year.

The common objection is the concept of "lock-in", but in actuality you've usually locked in a better price and should definitely have some performance and cancellation "escape hatch" options in any contract. Unless it's a totally different category or technology, I challenge you to find any service that you pay less for now than 5 years ago.

If you're worried about multiple year contracts with that shady LLC or new startup, then that means you shouldn't be doing business with them anyway. Don't be the usual office monkey doing the same tricks over and over. <u>Stop blindly doing one-year contracts and start reviewing multi-year options and discounts.</u>

Chapter 21: Using Unvetted IT Support is Willful Neglect

Although laws have yet to be passed, managed IT services must follow regulations for privacy and security as required by industry leaders like Microsoft and Google, as well as the current political climate.

Encryption is the main safe harbor against data breach, compliance penalties, and other litigation. In the event of a lost or stolen laptop, encryption of the hard drive means the data can't be accessed simply by installing a new operating system. As a safe harbor, businesses also don't have to report the loss publicly to customers or authorities in regulated industries like banking and medical.

However, a data breach from using unvetted IT support is considered willful neglect with average imposed penalties ranging from $10,000 to at least $50,000 by credit card companies and/or various Federal Agencies. For healthcare or banking and their business associates, these penalties may be assessed daily. If you're thinking that you're not a public organization or in a regulated industry, then be advised that under the Fair and Accurate Credit Transactions Act (FACTA) of 2003, the Federal Trade Commission is developing a similar fine schedule for ALL businesses that improperly dispose of employee or customer information leading to identity theft.

Here are the 5 criteria you should demand for vetted IT support:

1) **C Corporation.** These are the only entities with ownership that may be verified by the Secretary of State for the security and privacy of your data. For instance, Limited Liability Company (LLC) may be owned by felons, competitors, or foreign entities with no public record of ownership.

2) **Trademark and Patent.** What does an IT service provider really have to offer you without registered intellectual property at the U. S. Patent and Trademark Office (USPTO)? With a protected name and tagline, you know they are established with aligned motivations to your business goals like our trademark Streamline Your Technology® to reduce complexity and avoid risk. Using our patent-pending methodology also shows proven process versus "winging it" or guessing with some questionable steps from the Internet.

3) **Competency.** A Gold Competency by manufacturer such as our Microsoft Gold Cloud competency is required by approved specialization for the highest level of skills that is audited by Microsoft and published publicly at <u>partnercenter.microsoft.com</u>. Sliver competencies for Microsoft require limited or no on-going training with just three reference customers per year and should be avoided by customers as high risk with limited experience. This fact is true for other industry leaders.

4) **Compliance.** Although much of the IT industry will likely remain unregulated for cabling contractors to application developers, the managed IT services industry is now effectively regulated because of the privacy and security requirements required industry leaders like Microsoft, Google, and Amazon. Vetted IT support firms publish publicly annual Compliance Checklists and Executive Summary Risk Assessments. Basic Business Associate Agreements do not meet compliance verification. Failure to perform compliance training or maintain regulation policies and procedures is a disregard for customer privacy and data security.

5) **Published Authority.** A #1 best-selling cybersecurity book, like "Easy Prey" substantiates expertise. Just like tenured professors, you want experts with years of learning and implementation that have no qualms about sharing their knowledge versus incompetent novices googling for the answers.

In this era of fake news, the aspect all the above share is attribution to a reputable source. None of these criteria are paid advertising either. For the first time in the history of the IT support industry, there are real barriers to entry which protect clients from being swindled.

Chapter 22: Advice Managed IT Services Clients Should Demand Quarterly

The underlying critical aspect of managed IT services is providing business acumen to make informed decisions to improve the bottom line. There is no shortage of "solutions" to buy from sales people and there are ample technologists to implement. However, few organizations provide and justify business advice using proven practices. Since the technology industry is unregulated, virtually everyone is trying to build their own model with a common component of a quarterly meeting to review status and prove worth.

Unfortunately, most of the players don't understand the basic promises of managed services:

- Streamlining technology to reduce complexity and improve business productivity.

- Maintaining operations for less cost and risk for services and products versus growing a staff with related support infrastructure and management.

- Guiding business decisions for competitive advantage and business continuity using solid process, documentation, and education.

Truthfully, few technical organizations have actually adapted from the hourly staffing and products sales of the 1990's. It's no wonder that these same vendors don't understand what to provide for customers in a quarterly review. The following promises are what managed services customers should demand quarterly:

1. **Meet with management.** You're a key employee or a shareholder yourself, so you should meet with the CEO

or a Vice President from your managed service provider. This is not a sales call and you don't need something fixed by an engineer. The spend is in the thousands per year and your service provider should be just as committed and accountable to the relationship.

2. **Talk business.** A regular evaluation of your technology stance is not an account representative's Quarterly Business Review to make another sales call and fill out a satisfaction survey. In fact, modern service providers have no commission sales personnel. What you should get is a snapshot of your situation and some actionable recommendations from someone with enough authority to respond to your needs.

3. **See the big picture.** Talking about an abstract concept is nothing like seeing it. All customers should have a *logical* overview diagram consisting of where they stand today and what the image will look like in the future. Highly technical details are not as important as labeling major components and risk points over time.

4. **Realize that the model works.** There should be no discussion of rollover hours as you should always be in budget with flat cost. Expect an Executive Summary that shows overall health and uptime, problem devices, high-level account of activity, and comparison from previous periods. This deliverable should not be absently e-mailed to you to figure out. Just like an x-ray or legal brief, a degreed and certified professional should explain the results.

5. **Stay five years ahead.** You may not want to run the latest and greatest technology, but you should always have a rolling five-year technology forecast to know when to budget for needed upgrades and maintenance. More importantly, the forecast can be used to analyze additional growth and alternate strategies using new technology.

6. **Know immediate risks and action items.** Annually, each quarter should be identified with objectives, decisions, and outcomes. The game is understanding what's coming and using other tools like a forecast to make decisions or change direction entirely. The proactive communication and business review using gathered data provides real accountability and a record of action.

7. **Understand problem areas.** While most services providers have some sort of case management, very few do anything other than provide a listing. Customers should get a breakdown of cases by category and the service provider should analyze and review with you to eliminate recurring problems through education, new process, or depreciated products.

8. **Leverage improvements.** Forget the blatant brags like "we're the leading whatever on some important list". Service providers should be consistently telling what they've done to improve service for YOU such as self-service case entry, on-demand document access to client folders, real-time network status, and new knowledgebase updates.

9. **Acquire regular guidance.** Unfortunately, the biggest blind spot for most staff is learning new technology with little or no training. Prominent managed service providers today provide weekly blog posts to answer customer questions (not promotional web spam), as well as regular events to experience possible ways to utilize the latest technology without a sales pitch.

10. **Learn new concepts or strategy.** A free mouse pad or pen is a nice trinket, but major considerations customers should get quarterly is a personalized technology updates. Some pivotal technology could possibly change the outlook of your business for good or bad. Whether you choose to adopt

such ideas or not, you get early discovery to make your own decisions and plot your own course.

A quarterly meeting should be a <u>personalized business discussion</u> solely to give value to customers in about an hour and has nothing to do with sales. If you're regularly haggling over hours or grumbling about the performance of your service provider, then they've failed to communicate – much less deliver on promises.

Chapter 23: Stop Email and Web Surfing from Killing Business

In a recent Huffington Post survey, workers estimated they spent 3 hours per day checking e-mail. Likewise, a new poll by Forbes reveals that employees spend 1 to 3 hours wasting time surfing the web. With half the day squandered, it's no wonder it takes forever to finish projects and routine tasks – and customer service must really be lacking.

It's time to start taking back the work week and it starts with management. **Even a 15-minute improvement in process is approximately 100 hours in more productivity per year per employee.** Similarly, with cloud computing, Internet speed is a needed asset to effectively do business.

The problem with e-mail is that it is the fax of the 90's. You don't know if it was delivered or even read, and you don't know when to expect a response. Remember, e-mail was meant to be faster and cheaper than sending a letter or important contract, not a replacement for every other application or business need.

Unfortunately, the web is a dangerous place and even savvy Internet users are easy prey for ransomware that could cripple business. No one likes restrictions, but there is a medium between technology controls and business approach.

12 Tips for Solving Email Overload and Web Abuse

1) **Lead by example.** Stop using email as the primary channel for corporate or team communications. Tasks are assigned on a calendar or case management system. Spurious questions should be Instant Messaging (IM) only to eliminate the file, forward, or deletion required

of email conversations. Abide by the same web controls for pornography or shopping as your staff. Remember, management of any organization are the #1 target for computer criminals and often at highest risk with no controls for computer usage.

2) **Culture.** In our office, it's known that I don't want your e-mail, unless you have a deliverable or you're sending a meeting request. If I'm online, instant message me. Sure, you can go to YouTube, but sexually explicit, illegal, distasteful, or malicious sites are blocked.

3) **Calendar and/or Task Driven.** Every job has a daily routine with duties that must get done. Instead of addictively responding to every e-mail, turn off alerts and sounds for each message. Shift important tasks to reminders on your calendar and focus on completion. Your sense of accomplishment and self-worth will rise. Then you can set a few 15-minute timeframes throughout the day to get your email fix.

4) **Data Breach Education.** For less than what you pay for coffee service or office supplies, you can have your staff annually trained on appropriate computer use, what to avoid on social media, and how to spot email phishing with weekly reminders.

5) **Logon Disclaimer.** Regardless of culture, people need to understand that anything they do on a computer is recorded. At work, management can specify only business use and will review files and communication. Without regular

acknowledgement by a logon banner, any computer use or sanction policy may be nullified by an employee stating computer use was never discussed after initial hiring. Example disclaimer (consult an attorney for specific language):

This private computer system including all files and uses is the property of Matrixforce and intended for authorized business use only. By using this system, the user indicates awareness of and consents to monitoring and inspection of any uses of this system and all files on this system. Unauthorized or improper use of this system may result in administrative disciplinary action and civil and criminal penalties. LOG OFF IMMEDIATELY if you do not agree to the conditions stated in this warning.

6) **External Email Warning.** With the abundance of public social media information about key employees, hackers regularly use spear phishing techniques to send personalized e-mail scams to get account credentials or financial information. An external e-mail warning at the top of the message about that wire transfer from your boss makes the sham obvious at a glance. Example:

NOTICE: THIS EMAIL IS FROM AN EXTERNAL SOURCE. DO NOT OPEN ATTACHMENTS OR CLICK ON LINKS FROM UNKNOWN SENDERS OR UNEXPECTED EMAIL.

7) **Simple Rules.** Never reply to email flames and always handle complaints via phone. Use BCC instead of CC to eliminate unnecessary reply all threads. If it takes more than 5 minutes to

compose, then an e-mail is not the right type of communication.

8) **Focused Inbox.** Instead of idly turning it off, use the new artificial intelligence to help you handle e-mail. Focus is the important e-mail and Other is the newsletters, promotions, etc. Just right-click any message to move to Focus or Other tab to train your robot on your preferences.

9) **Email Retention.** Email is your highest risk for data breach, reputation damage, and legal action. From executives of major corporations to politicians like Hillary Clinton, they've all been burned by lack of email retention. Important documents and information should be saved in departmental files or organization databases. Enabling retention like 5 years for key employees and 2 years for other staff reduces liability and inefficient hoarding of messages.

10) **Encrypted Email and Websites.** If you have an attachment, modern email systems use keywords like CONFIDENTIAL or ENCRYPTED in the subject to send out of public view to protect the sender and recipient from data breach. Using InPrivate or Incognito mode and going only to websites showing the lock icon or HTTPS prevents any third-party tracking of web browsing, while ensuring legitimate sites.

11) **Block Malicious Attachments and Sites.** Virtually all SPAM filters have the capability to block executable programs in any files, including compressed ZIP before they can be delivered to your inbox. Drive by downloads that don't require

you to click on a link or pop-up are how most networks are taken hostage by hackers and can be prevented by most web filtering.

12) **Computer Use and Sanction Policy.** According to the SANS Institute, less than 30% of companies have a computer use policy and those that do have little or no way to enforce it. To compound matters, most organizations also don't have a sanction policy for computer use outlining how workplace violations are handled or specific causes for termination. Examples abound on the Internet, but the best starting point is documenting what automated controls you can enforce. As always, contact an attorney for review.

Chapter 24: Evading the Ransomware Epidemic

Ransomware is a type of malware that is covertly installed on a computer without knowledge or intention of the user. Ransomware restricts access to the infected computer system by encrypting data and demands that the user pay a ransom to the malware cyber criminals to unencrypt the data.

The FBI recently reported incidents of ransomware on the rise with consumers and small businesses as the favorite targets because of less sophisticated security. In addition, the Department of Homeland Security has issued a recent alert on emerging ransomware variants (https://www.us-cert.gov/ncas/alerts/TA16-091A).

These cyber-attacks are so sophisticated that computer users may become infected from legitimate websites, without clicking on links on a page or in an e-mail. Further, new strains are corrupting server and workstation operating systems, **requiring full re-installation of systems AND restoration of data to replace encrypted files**.

> *There is no one method or tool that will completely protect you or your organization from a ransomware attack.*
> – James Trainor, FBI Cyber Division Assistant Director

Ransomware Attacks

Last spring, NBC news reported that ransomware attacks cost businesses over $200 million in just the first three months of 2016. As ransomware attacks escalate, ransom prices vary depending on the ransomware variant and the price or exchange rates of digital currencies. Thanks to the perceived anonymity offered by cryptocurrencies, ransomware operators commonly specify ransom payments in bitcoins. Recent ransomware variants have also listed alternative payment options such as iTunes and Amazon gift cards. It should be noted, however, that paying for the ransom does not guarantee that users will get the decryption key or unlock tool required to regain access to the infected system or hostage files.

Hospitals, financial institutions, and small business are particularly easy targets and big pay days for cyber criminals. Because of compliance regulations, each of these groups must also pay government penalties and disclose security violations to protect the privacy of customers. Unfortunately, the notoriety only gives more incentive for cyber criminals.

Mac 'Ransomware' Attack Exposes Vulnerability of Apple Users (*NY Times*) – For the first time, security experts say, a dangerous form of software called "ransomware" has successfully targeted a Mac operating system, piercing an image of safety that Apple customers had long enjoyed.

Hospital Declares 'Internal State of Emergency' After Ransomware Infection (*KrebsOnSecurity*) – A Kentucky hospital says it is operating in an "internal state of emergency" after a ransomware attack rattled around inside its networks, encrypting files on computer systems and holding the data on them hostage unless and until the hospital pays up.

Big Paydays Force Hospitals to Prepare for Ransomware Attacks (*NBC News*) – One of the most extreme cases took place in February, when Hollywood Presbyterian Medical Center handed over $17,000 to hackers who took over its systems.

Congress warned about cybersecurity after attempted ransomware attack on House (*TechCrunch*)– Congressional gridlock can usually be blamed on stubborn representatives and senators. But a new string of ransomware attacks on the House of Representatives could stall legislation more effectively than party infighting or a filibuster.

'Ransomware' crime wave growing (*CNN Money*)– It began with an early morning phone call and instant fear for the technology director of Horry County, South Carolina's school district.

Maryland hospital: Ransomware success wasn't IT department's fault (*Arstechnica*) – MedStar, the health network of 10 Maryland hospitals struck by a ransomware attack last week possibly due to failed system patches.

Ransomware alert issued by US and Canada following recent attacks (*Sophos*) – The plague doesn't appear to be going away anytime soon. Why should it? It's proving a lucrative swindle for cyber thieves.

'Ransomware' Attacks to Grow in 2016 (*Security Magazine*) – The number of cyberattacks where malware holds user data "hostage" is expected to grow in 2016 as hackers target more companies and advanced software is able to compromise more types of data, according to a report from Intel Corp.'s McAfee Labs.

Ransomware attacks quadrupled in Q1 2016 (*Fedscoop*) – Ransomware has taken off in 2016, with attacks in the first quarter coming at quadruple the rate seen last year, according to figures from a leading security vendor.

Ransomware: Lucrative, fast growing, hard to stop (*CNBC*) – The hackers behind recent high-profile ransomware attacks on U.S. hospitals are using business methods that might be familiar to some Silicon Valley start-ups.

In the fight to protect customers from cybercrime, ransomware attacks are considered especially heinous. This article is based upon true events. Any names, dates, and locations have been changed to protect the innocent.

Ransomware Steals Independence Day

The hack began at approximately 3:45 AM on Tuesday, July 5th, 2016. Before 6AM it was over and the network was fully encrypted by cybercriminals, except for one functioning server. Every other server, plus all workstations that were powered on were rendered useless. If you could log on at all, the operating system was now unlicensed with a broken profile. Most of the necessary system files and any data files had .LOL extensions (such as somefile.docx.lol). So, no programs work and the LOL files cannot be opened (even on an uninfected computer) without the decryption key. Most folders contained a "JOKE" ransom note named "how to get data.txt" with the contents below:

> *JOKE*
>
> *Hello boys and girls! Welcome to our high school "GPCODE"!*
>
> *If you are reading this text (read this very carefully, if you can read), this means that you have missed a lesson about safety and YOUR PC HACKED !!! Dont worry guys – our school specially for you! The best teachers have the best recommendations in the world! Feedback from our students, you can read here:*
>
> *1)http://forum.kaspersky.com*
> *2)http://forum.drweb.com 3)http://forum.eset,com*
> *4)www.forospyware.com*

As you see- we trust their training, only we have special equipment(cryptor.exe and decryptor.exe) and only here you will get an unforgettable knowledge!

The lesson costs not expensive. Calculate the time and money you spend on recovery. Time is very expensive, almost priceless. We think that it is cheaper to pay for the lesson and never repeat the mistakes. We guarantee delivery of educational benefits(decryptor.exe). First part(cryptor.exe)you

have received

SERIOUSLY

Your important files (photos, videos, documents, archives, databases, backups, etc.) which were crypted with the strongest military cipher RSA1024 and AES. No one can `t help you to restore files without our decoder. Photorec, RannohDecryptor etc repair tools are useless and can destroy your files irreversibly.

If you want to restore files – send e-mail to gpcode@gp2mail.com with the file "how to get data.txt" and 1-2 encrypted files less than 5 MB. PLEASE USE PUBLIC MAIL LIKE YAHOO or GMAIL.

You will receive decrypted samples and our conditions how you `ll get the decoder. Follow the instructions to send payment.

P.S. Remember, we are not scammers. We don `t need your files. After one month all your files and keys will be deleted. Oops! Just send a request immediately after infection. All data will be restored absolutelly. Your warranty – decrypted samples and positive feedbacks from previous users.

The typos and poor grammar are either intentional or an obvious product of English not being their primary language. Even today, if you Google for this virus or ransomware, there is very little published. Most results are bogus or blatant pitches from anti-malware or backup tools. To date, no anti-malware has been effective in preventing ransomware. Purchasing backup software after the fact is useless.

Just like a pond or swimming pool filled with algae, the only course of action for a compromised network is to drain it. You fully reinstall all workstations and servers. Then you restore data from backup. Alternatively, you can pay the ransom. For customers who discover they don't have adequate backup, paying the ransom may be the only alternative. However, the process to pay the ransom is neither quick nor easy.

Paying Ransom with Bitcoin

There was one old physical accounting server that was soon to be de-commissioned. Typical for a disaster, another vendor was in the middle of performing a migration to a new version of the accounting software on a virtual server. The new virtual server was toast. While we were confident in our backup, if the files could be decrypted it would save considerable restoration time. As we began to rebuild the world, we also took a gamble on paying the ransom.

The recommendation from authorities is never to pay the ransom. The FBI recommends that you contact them and they will handle the investigation. Most business owners don't report ransomware infections out of the concern for a public record and the fact that a formal investigation does nothing to get your systems running or data restored. This customer was not in a regulatory industry and had no requirement to report the breach.

If you're not familiar with Bitcoin, it's the favorite digital currency of cybercriminals because it does not use traditional banks to come under government scrutiny. Although bitcoins may be generated or mined by specialized computational machines, most bitcoins today are purchased by cash or wire transfer from banks. Many people think of bitcoins as a commodity like gold. However, the value of bitcoin is much more volatile.

We created a new Yahoo account and sent a message to the specified address with a couple of encrypted data files. Gp2mail.com is hosted by Cloud Flare in San Francisco according to the American Registry of Internet Numbers (ARIN). However, the domain registrar is in Shanghai and contact information for the domain is a fake U.S. address with an invalid state of DK.

It took 5 hours for the criminals to respond. The reply was as follows and the two files attached were indeed decrypted:

> *Sorry for delay.*
> *Here is decrypted sample. Decryptors price in first two weeks is 0.3 bitcoin.*
> *In next weeks – 1 BTC. Time is determined by key from "how to get*
> *data.txt", this key contains exact time of infection. Pay and save your*
> *money and time. Warrantee is your decrypted samples and GPCODE`s 10 year*
> *history.*
> *After payment you `ll get the decryptor.exe in 2-12 hours and all your*
> *files will be decrypted automatically.*
> *If i don `t send decryptor for you, who will pay to me in the future?*
> *Get additional information and join to discussion about GPCODE here*
> *http://www.bleepingcomputer.com/forums/t/581458 /all-file-extensions-changed-to-lol/*
> *See this links to find bitcoins*
> *http://howtobuybitcoins.info/.*
> *Here https://coincafe.com/legal.php#_"Ransomware Policy" you can get full*
> *support for ransomware victims. This way is preferable.*
> *Also usable for paypal https://paxful.com/buy-bitcoin/paypal*
> *If you are ready to pay, send payment to this bitcoin address-*
> *1Lftk171zMH1AY1DSdbP7qcnNNj1DiUz3y*
> *Please send me notice,when you `ll send payment.*

You can Google the exchange rate for bitcoin. At the time, 0.3 bitcoins were valued at $246. Building a new virtual server, restoring the SQL databases, and having the accounting vendor perform an emergency migration would take at least 12 hours. In comparison to the restoration effort, the ransom would be a small price to pay.

Throughout the ransom process, you have little expectation or control of when the cybercriminals will respond or the length time to process a bitcoin order. It can easily take 4-5 days to simply purchase bitcoin, transfer to cybercriminals, and get a decryption program in return. While you may be able to decrypt systems and data, some workstations and servers will have boot problems requiring reinstall regardless.

The process for purchasing bitcoin is shockingly invasive. While the cybercriminals get to remain anonymous, you must give up your entire identity. To purchase bitcoin, you must submit:

1. A photo of the front and back of your driver's license.

2. A selfie of you holding your driver's license beside your face.

3. Your Social Security Number.

4. A copy of a utility or cable bill with the same address as your driver's license.

All of this information is required to just setup an account with a bitcoin exchange like CoinCafe. Supposedly, bitcoin exchanges in the U.S. are required to record these personal details in accordance with the Patriot Act. Bear in mind that these organizations are not regulated or backed by the Federal Reserve.

The next day our account was verified. Instead of providing unknown bitcoin exchange operators full access to draft a bank account, it's common to FedEx cash. Since the exchange rate is volatile, $20 – $50 more than the needed amount should be sent. Again, you must take a picture of the cash with the order number and upload it. Sometime the next day, you order is

processed and you have a bitcoin amount in your digital
wallet. You can then transfer a specified amount to the bitcoin
wallet address on the ransom and then e-mail the thieves about
the pending transaction. The following day, we received this
message with a link to download the decryption program:

Sorry for delay.
Extract file from ZIP,rename(add to file) *.exe
extension (must
be decryptor.exe), run decryptor and wait for
the message -Done! .it`s need a lot of
time. all your files will be decrypted automatically.
Better
way, if you have some doubts- dismount your
hard drive and connect it to another
PC as volume. After this step run decryptor and check
files.
if some files are not decrypted
1) check "how to get data.txt" -may
be in this files keys are different?
2) Probably you have issues with read-write
permissions in
some folders or discs.Try to delete LOL!
extension manually and open file(if
file are good,then use AntRenamer for another
files).Try run
decryptor with admin rights. Also check file
names in folder-may be you have files
with the same name?
3) send me a letter with undecrypted sample
4) dont use simple passwords, create rules and policies
for each
user,restrict programs for run, set password on
antivirus, disable admin rights, create cloud
backups. Please reply to me, when you get
decryptor. I hope that learn was useful for
you. Bonus- now you know about bitcoins.

We didn't have the luxury to wait for all the delays and bureaucracy. By the time the hackers responded with the decryption program, operations had been restored to a new accounting server. The old accounting server had been disconnected from the network and the decryption program did unencrypt the files. However, a required reboot made the server restart continuously. Even attempted repair of the operating system would not fix the problem. <u>Our gamble ultimately failed as the ransomware decryption corrupted critical boot files beyond repair.</u>

Ransomware Cause and Prevention

Just because you have regularly patched systems with stringent firewall security, it's only a matter of time before you face the same fate described above – unless you take some extra precautions. Virtually every business has some type of remote desktop or virtual private network access to their systems. Modern ransomware attacks are performed by foreign state sponsored hackers that probe for weak user account security. Targeted company users are fully researched through corporate websites and social media.

All it takes is some employees using weak or easily guessed passwords from the wealth of information online and it's all over. Investigating afterwards, a couple of staff members had very generic passwords. A brute force password attack took literally no time to access the VPN server. Once logged on, the hackers downloaded their favorite security tools to begin to enumerate the local server administrator. The hackers then created backdoors, cracked the domain admin password, crippled the firewall, and finally encrypted the entire network. Web filtering and up-to-date anti-virus and patching didn't matter.

The only way to prevent ransomware attacks is threefold:

1. Annual staff training on data breach with acknowledgement of the top 20 security policies and procedures, as well as an annual risk assessment.

2. Roaming network management to prevent traditional malware from phoning home and to immediately identify traffic from a compromised device.

3. Device management with multi-factor authentication (password you know and a text sent to your phone i.e. something you have and something you know) to prevent account hacks and provide selective remote wipe/lock on mobile or stationary devices.

Naïve or arrogant computer users foolishly believe that they are protected from ransomware with anti-virus or firewalls, or know enough to avoid infection that could never happen to them. However, the only way to prevent ransomware is a combination of new cyber security, on-going security breach, and stringent device controls. Ransomware prevention is often less than what most organizations spend on coffee and office supplies per year per employee or approximately $1,000 - 3,000 per employee per year according to 2017 report by Business Wire.

Chapter 25: Roadmap for Data Breach in Banking, Healthcare, and Related Industries

5 Data Breach Predictions for 2018

As reported June 2017 by Bloomberg, the Trump administration laid out an overhaul of bank rules from the Treasury Department report that exempt small to mid-sized banks under $10 billion in assets from the Dodd-Frank stress tests, Volcker Rule, and similar other rules. Beyond banking, most companies are just now putting data breach preparedness on their radar.

Staying ahead of emerging threats requires constant vigilance, because of the increasing sophistication of cybercriminals. Much like the health industry, financial organizations outside of banking like insurance and accounting are now required to have an assigned security officer. These predictions are derived from the Experian 2017 Data Breach Industry Forecast:

1. Tsunami password breaches will bring about required Multi-Factor Authentication (MFA).

   Underwater earthquakes cause violent shaking of the seafloor triggering devastating tsunami waves around coastal areas. Since much of the world is connected through the Internet like the oceans, data breaches from weak passwords often come in huge waves as hackers sell passwords in bulk on the dark web. With breached passwords sold multiple times and since users often reuse passwords, companies that didn't experience a first-hand data breach become the target of repeated unauthorized logons. Multi-factor authentication where you enter a password you know and a 6-digit text to the phone that you have will be mandatory for any systems with Personally Identifiable Information (PII).

2. Organized crime will surpass foreign state cyber-attacks in a move to cash in on unsuspecting consumers and unsophisticated small businesses.

   Governments have yet to adopt the Digital Geneva Convention outlined by Microsoft's President and Chief Legal Officer, Brad Smith. However, political pressure on nation-state cyberattacks have decentralized to fund crime syndicates with consumers and small businesses as continued collateral damage. Beyond cybersecurity insurance, all firms should invest in data breach training, cybersecurity monitoring, and mobile device management.

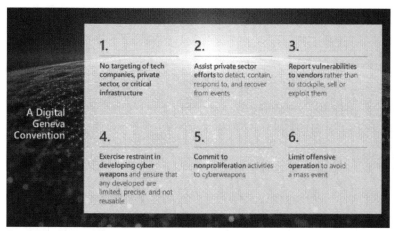

Source: Microsoft

3. Business associates of healthcare and professional service organizations will be the most targeted sector of emerging sophisticated attacks.

   While most vendors are providing a due diligence packet or a business associate agreement, most of these entities are small businesses that are not receiving an annual third-party risk assessment or training employees on data breach and implementing regulation compliant policies / procedures. Regulated firms must require a signed Compliance Checklist by a business associate officer and an Executive Summary of the latest Risk Assessment.

4. Bitcoin will remain the dominate currency demanded by hackers with higher ransom costs for victims.

   Goldman Sachs July 2017 Analyst Report shows Bitcoin price to soon hit $4,000 for one Bitcoin mainly because of increase in global demand and usage. The decentralized and unregulated government currency allows multiple Bitcoin accounts or wallets anonymously setup around the world with automated rules to transfer to another Bitcoin exchange in another country within seconds.

5. Ransomware will become the #1 disaster bankrupting businesses after a data breach.

   Each year, the Small Business Administration estimate remains stable that 40% of businesses go bankrupt after any type of natural or man-made disaster – often because of lacking backup. With the advent ransomware, owners will experience bankruptcy and catastrophic reputation damage.

Reputation Damage Calculator

Top Concerns: security breach reasons, penalties, security costs, and future prevention.

Scenarios	Value	Units
Outage Duration	8	Hours
Employees Affected	12	Employees
Productivity Loss	100%	Percentage
Revenue non-recoverable	100%	Percentage
Average Employee Cost	$22	Hourly
Average Employee Revenue	$104	Hourly
Intangible Cost	$11	Hourly
Productivity Loss	$3,168	Violation
Revenue Loss	$9,984	Violation
Intangible Loss	$0	Violation
Compliance Penalties	$10,000	Incident
New Security Products	$12,000	Incident
Total Loss	**$35,152**	

Unknowns	Matrixforce
Damaged Reputation	System Assurance
Permanent Loss	Guaranteed Uptime
Compliance Penalties	Guaranteed Response
Contract Defaults	50% Average Savings
Opportunity Loss	Performance Reporting
Technical Inexperience	Vetted IT Support
Competitive Disadvantage	Numerous Clients

What Is Cybersecurity and Compliance Risk Management?

Security guidelines can be confusing and compliance expensive, whether HIPAA, SOX, GLBA, PCI, or FACTA. Yet there are simple and inexpensive tips you can take to secure financial and personally identifiable information. The first thing to realize is that security is a process and takes time to implement. No business becomes "compliant" overnight. There is no magic product to purchase or book to read that will make your organization instantly regulation compliant.

Iterative Risk Management Process

At the core of any cybersecurity is a process called Risk Management, which is not as confusing as it sounds. This an oversimplified definition of Risk Management but it illustrates that the process is one that is repeated over and over.

Risk Management

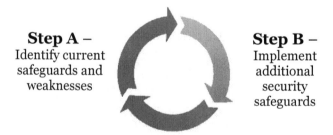

Step A –
Identify current safeguards and weaknesses

Step B –
Implement additional security safeguards

Step C – Go back to Step A

Step A – Identify how you are currently protecting information and identify current weakness in your protection.

Step B – Implement additional security safeguards to better protect information

Step C – Go back to Step A

Risk Assessment

How do you identify how you are protecting information and your weaknesses? Most cybersecurity compliance rules call for organizations to perform a Risk Assessment. Let's look at a simplified definition:

Step 1 – Identify where information is stored (Line-Of-Business Application, CRM system, email, etc.)

Step 2 - Identify threats to information (employee loses a laptop with financial or personally identifiable information, fire destroys your systems, a customer is sent another customer's financials, etc.)

Step 3 – Assess how you are currently protecting information (backing up your systems on a nightly basis, using encrypted email to send sensitive information, using anti-virus to protect your systems from viruses, etc.)

Step 4 – Determine your risk for each of the threats that were identified in Step 2. You determine your risk by looking at how likely something is to happen and the impact if it does happen.

Step 5 – Determine additional protections to lower the risk. Using the previous example, if you determined the risk of a fire would be high because you are not backing up your data, then implementing a nightly offsite data backup would lower your risk.

6 Easy and Economical Tips to Protect Data

Most data breaches happen due to lost or stolen portable devices. Portable devices include laptops, USB drives, CDs, DVDs, Backup tapes/drives, Smartphones, etc. These portable devices can hold hundreds or thousands of records. There are a few simple and inexpensive ways of protecting portable devices to minimize the risk of losing patient information. Four of the tips will focus on portable devices and the remaining two tips will review how good password controls can protect critical information.

Tip #1 – Encrypt all laptops

The official description of encryption is that it is a Safe Harbor under all compliance regulations, but I like to call it the "get out of jail free card". If you lose a laptop with confidential information and it is encrypted you can act, for regulation compliance purposes as though it was never lost. Bitlocker is included free with Windows 10. Encryption usually has no noticeable effect on using the laptop and only requires a password or pin to be entered when you first startup the laptop.

Tip # 2 – Minimize the use of portable devices and the amount of data

To reduce the risk of confidential information stored on a portable device, make it a practice to not use portable devices. Raise your staff awareness of the risks of portable devices. Write a memo or send an email to all employees stating that the use of portable devices to store customer information is frowned upon. If employees must use portable devices, then the amount of customer or employee information stored on the devices should be only the minimum needed.

If USB drives must be used then only use encrypted USB drives. While it is true that encrypted USB drives are more expensive than non-encrypted USB drives, the cost is not prohibitive and usually around $25.

Tip #3 – Encrypt all backup tapes and drives

If you are still using tapes or backup drives for your data, then ensure that they are encrypted. Backup tapes or drives hold all your data. If a backup tape or drive is lost or stolen, you could have a very large data breach. Most backup software supports data encryption, but it must be enabled first.

Tip #4 – Smartphone startup password and encryption

Smartphones such as iPhone, Android, Windows Phone and BlackBerry may contain confidential customer and employee information. If the phone is lost or stolen, protect your smartphone ahead of time by ensuring that a start-up password, inactivity timeout, and encryption have been enabled to reduce the likelihood that confidential information is compromised.

Tip #5 – Implement good password controls

Passwords are the key to protecting systems. Encourage employees to use complex passwords that have upper and lower case letters, special symbols such as "@!$%&", and numbers. Passwords should not be written down on sticky notes and stuck on monitors or put under the keyboard. Accounts should be locked 3 – 5 failed password attempts to thwart hackers from unauthorized access.

Tip #6 – Enable Two-Factor Authentication

You've seen it on Gmail and Facebook. With a click of a check box, you can enable a text with a pin code sent to your phone when you log into these services. The something you know and something you have paradigm prevents hackers from using automated scripts to guess your password. For many systems and applications, two-factor authentication is free.

Wrap-up

These are a few simple and inexpensive tips that you can easily implement to protect customer information and help you toward security compliance. Following these tips will go a long way toward providing increased protection of your confidential information.

8 Important Facts to Know About HIPAA

There is a lot to know about HIPAA and the HIPAA Security Rule. There are multiple steps and numerous security precautions that need to be implemented. Although the process to comply with HIPAA might seem overwhelming, no organization becomes compliant overnight and an iterative process is required for compliance. The following are 7 things that you must know about HIPAA security.

1. **HIPAA is not optional**

HIPAA compliance is not optional for covered entities like healthcare providers (even small practices) or business associates such as IT consultants and law firms or accountants. According to Wikipedia

> *Security Rule*
> *The Final Rule on Security Standards was*
> *issued on February 20, 2003. It took effect*
> *on April 21, 2003 with a compliance date of*
> *April 21, 2005 for most covered entities and*
> *April 21, 2006 for "small plans"*

On the other hand, if you are a contractor or business associate of a covered entity you were previously only loosely required to comply with the HIPAA Security Rule. Business associates were required to sign business associate agreements that contractually required them to protect patient information. That has now changed with the release of the HIPAA Omnibus Final Rule that makes business associates directly liable for compliance with the HIPAA Security Rule:

Make business associates of covered entities directly liable for compliance with certain of the HIPAA Privacy and Security Rules requirements.

2. Iterative HIPAA Risk Management Process

At the core of HIPAA security is a process called Risk Management. As covered in previous sections, Risk Management identifies current protections and weaknesses, implements better safeguards, and starts over each year to continually audit and improve.

3. You must perform a Risk Assessment

The HIPAA Security Rule and HIPAA Omnibus Final Rule mandates that all covered entities and business associates perform a Risk Assessment to determine how electronic protected health information (ePHI) is being protected and to recommend additional safeguards. The output of a Risk Assessment provides valuable insight into vulnerabilities to ePHI and how ePHI can be better protected.

If an organization is audited by the Department of Health and Human Services (HHS), one of the first questions is asked would be "where is a copy of your latest Risk Assessment?" Fines will automatically be assessed if you don't have one or produce something that is outdated or incomplete.

4. Encryption is your friend

Think of encryption as "an unbreakable password". Information that is encrypted is safe and secure and cannot be accessed without the encryption password or key. Although encryption is not a requirement under the HIPAA Security Rule, it does provide a "safe harbor" of dramatically reducing liability in the event of a security incident like a lost or stolen laptop or desktop. Just remember to keep the encryption USB key or password separate from the device. In other words, don't put the password on a sticky note on the laptop.

5. <u>You must train your employees on HIPAA Security</u>

The HIPAA Security Rule and HIPAA Omnibus Final Rule also mandate that covered entities and business associates setup a security awareness / training program for all workforce members to go through security training annually. In addition, the HIPAA Security Rule requires that employees be provided with ongoing security reminders throughout the year.

6. <u>You must have written policies and procedures</u>

The HIPAA Security Rule requires written policies and procedures which describe how ePHI is to be protected. It is not good enough to have policies and/or procedures that are generally used but not written down. Policies and procedures must be documented with verified distribution to employees including reported enforcement by your organization.

7. <u>Media disposal is one of the most forgotten risks</u>

While it should be one of your policies and procedures, people often forget that the leased copier or dead fax machine stores a copy of all documents copied or faxed. Just like an old smartphone or computer, the data must be wiped for disposal to prevent fraudulent use.

8. <u>You must have an incident response plan</u>

To be compliant with the HIPAA Security Rule and HIPAA Omnibus Final Rule, you must have a security incident response plan (SIRP) in place. A SIRP is a predefined plan that guides an organization through the steps which must be taken in the event of a security breach or incident:

1. **Define the incident** – What happened, when, who was involved, and when was it discovered?

2. **Stop the incident** – If a breach is discovered such as a lost smartphone, is found take the steps to disable or prevent further access, etc.

3. **Document the incident** –Clearly document all aspects of the incident from step 1 and 2.

4. **Determine who has been affected by the incident** – which patient records have been affected?

5. **Perform a risk assessment** – a risk assessment will determine if the breach has led to disclosure of ePHI. The outcome will determine next steps including any required notification steps.

6. **Notification** – notify appropriate individuals / agencies. Breaches affecting over 500 individuals require significantly more notifications. Individual patients and Health and Human Services (HHS) will need to be notified. In addition, local media may need to be notified as well.

7. **Provide guidance to prevent the incident from occurring again** – an important aspect of a security incident response plan is to ensure that the same incident does not happen in the future. Recommendations to increase security and reduce the risk of an incident are essential.

Leon Rodriguez, director of the Office of Civil Rights (OCR) at the Department of Health and Human Services, made it clear that organizations that have a SIRP in place and act quickly and decisively about large breaches will receive less severe or no monetary penalties. But organizations that do not act or correct issues related to a breach will receive much higher monetary penalties.

> *"One of the first things we look at is what did the entity do to analyze the root cause of the breach," he said "[And] what did it do to remedy the root causes. Huge points for the entity that acts decisively to deal with those issues, to identify the reasons for the breach".*

Conclusion

Hopefully you now have a better understanding of some of the things you need to do to comply with the HIPAA Security Rule. Remember, the process to comply with HIPAA is an iterative process. Each item that you address or implement gets you a step closer to being compliant.

Our Overwatch HIPAA security offers comprehensive and affordable service that can help you with:

- ✓ Performing a HIPAA risk assessment
- ✓ Writing your HIPAA security policies and procedures
- ✓ Training your employees and providing security reminders
- ✓ Implementing encryption to protect patient information
- ✓ Implementing a security incident response plan

HIPAA Compliance Roadmap

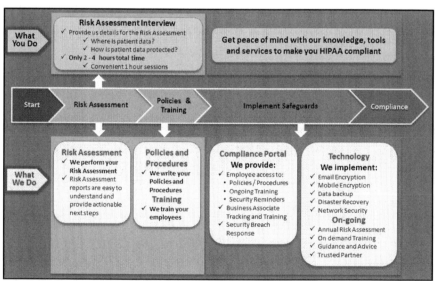

Source: Enertia Group

If you would like to learn more about our comprehensive Overwatch® HIPAA Cybersecurity service, feel free to contact us at sales@matrixforce.com.

Chapter 26: About Kevin Fream

KEVIN FREAM is CEO of Matrixforce, #1 Best-Selling cybersecurity author of *Easy Prey*, and the creator of the "Delta Method of Streamlining Technology™" He has appeared on ABC, NBC, CBS, and FOX News for cybersecurity and even Harvard Business School for thought leadership.

Kevin Fream brings twenty-five years of experience as a cyber security advisor to prospective customers. He specializes in helping business owners and leadership teams reduce technological complexity and avoid risk, with an emphasis on highlighting current compliance penalties that impact the viability of nearly every business. More cyber security insights, tools, and downloads may be accessed at Cyberprey.com.

While Kevin was completing his Bachelor of Science in Management Information Systems degree from the University of Tulsa, he landed a paid internship with DuPont. That early experience with one of the most security conscious organizations in the nation allowed him to go on to work nationwide with many other Fortune 500 firms.

Along the way, he noted that the local marketplace was riddled with suspect competencies, rude behavior, and relentless hourly billing. Mid-sized businesses of $5 million to $150 million in revenue seem to be particularly under-served and mistreated. As a result, Kevin formulated a distinct customer service strategy:

1) Assume the risk for customers by offering flat cost and demonstrating business justification. No one would be compensated for billable hours or selling products.

2) Train staff on rules of engagement and how to talk with customers in simple language, so that they can understand and control outcomes for information technology.

3) Specialize in Microsoft productivity and security solutions for annually audited expertise.

Today, Matrixforce has saved clients collectively over $500 million on technology services and products and is a top 100 Microsoft Gold Cloud Partner.

Keep up with the latest cybersecurity news and events at KevinFream.com

Chapter 27: How Does Your Computer Guy Stack Up?

Take the quiz and find out!

How can you tell if you're unknowingly receiving second-rate or abysmal service? How do you know your computer guy is doing everything practical to protect you from ransomware, data loss, or other disasters? Could the technician you use be putting your business in jeopardy through apathy and ineptitude?

If your computer guy doesn't score a "Yes" to every point, you're probably paying for substandard IT support.

☐ Are they vetted with verifiable ownership as a C Corporation with specialized competency and regulation compliance audited by authorities, using patented IT support and published expertise?

☐ Do they provide client access to their 7x25 network monitoring, so you can run reports on demand and ensure your systems are being maintained?

☐ Are they easy to reach during non-emergencies by answering the phone live and providing cell phone numbers for all contacts?

☐ Do they take on unknown risk with flat cost and easy to understand invoices without rollover hours or confusing billing items?

☐ Do they have a guaranteed response and guaranteed weekly system assurance?

☐ Do they proactively review your cases with you to identify and eliminate recurring problems?

☐ Do they have multiple technicians that are familiar with your system in case of illness, vacation, job change, or other unavailability?

☐ Do they provide a 5-year technology forecast so you have no surprises on future purchases or projects?

☐ Do they provide self-service and secure access to a System Plan for your network maintenance and disaster recovery, along with standard operating procedures for your applications and onboarding of employees?

☐ Do they understand the laws and regulations with on-going staff training that apply to your business?

Thank You

The first responsibility of a leader is to define reality. The last is to say thank you. In between, the leader is a servant.
- Max de Pree

It's my hope that these secrets to streamlining technology give you competitive advantage and help your business prosper. It's an honor and a privilege to share and give back.

Selecting an IT partner is not easy, but just as important as choosing a new doctor, lawyer, or CPA. You should only change IT support when you've lost faith in your current provider, but most business owners often don't inspect their IT until a major problem happens.

That's our trademark and mission at Matrixforce:

Streamlining technology to reduce complexity and avoid risk.

Less products for you to buy means less for us to support. Our win-win approach with mutually beneficial motivations lets us both focus on improving your business.

Thank you for taking the time to read this book.

If you have any questions about information technology, this book, or other related issues, please e-mail me at kfream@matrixforce.com or call me at (918) 622-1167.

Resources

Business Strategy and Cybersecurity

StreamliningTechnology.com – Site for this book and the launchpad more secrets and events.

Cyberprey.com – *"Easy Prey"* cybersecurity resources and downloads for the business reality of regulation compliance, penalties, and reputation damage.

Adroit.blog – Digital outcomes for business success with IT support and tips on inbound marketing for converting more customers.

Blog.matrixforce.com – Official blog of Matrixforce for the latest information on managed IT services, cloud computing, and cybersecurity.

Partnercenter.microsoft.com – Find a qualified Microsoft partner and get the latest incentives.

Microsoft.com/trustcenter – Comprehensive security resource and guidance by industry.

Pumpkinplan.com – Strategy to grow a remarkable business in any field.

Scalingup.com – How a few companies make it and the rest don't.

Office 365 Legal Agreements

Security is one of the main differentiators for Microsoft Office 365. Unfortunately, unless you know the terminology, it can be difficult to find legal agreement information for Office 365. The following is a list we've compiled in one place for quick search and review:

1. Microsoft Online Subscription Agreement. This document is the primary agreement between Microsoft and the entity purchasing online services that outlines: terms and conditions, use rights, Service Level Agreements, and pricing and payment.

2. Office 365 Service Level Agreement. The SLA provides service level commitment specification and outlines the financially backed guarantee.

3. Office 365 Trust Center. This link is a resource center for your toughest privacy and security questions.

4. Office 365 and CRM Online Data Processing Agreement*. Defense-in-depth approach to provide physical, logical, and data layers of security features and operational best practices.

5. Office 365 and CRM Online HIPAA/HITECH Business Associate Agreement*. Brief overview of regulation requirements with a detailed analysis of how Microsoft cloud services were built with methodologies that map to those requirements.

6. Office 365 and CRM Online Data Processing Agreement (with EU Standard Contractual Clauses)*. Authorities across Europe approve Microsoft's commitment to cloud services.

7. <u>Office 365 Security Amendment (for customers outside of Europe)</u>*. Straightforward guide to Microsoft's approach to protecting data.

*Office 365 administrator login credentials required

If you have an Office 365 subscription, you can logon to review and accept the <u>Optional Privacy and Security Contractual Supplements</u>.

Special Offer

Dear Reader,

Thank you for staying with me so far, but our journey is far from over.

1. **Invite me to speak at your next meeting or event**

   If you like what your read in this book or if you've see any of my segments on TV and other events, then please invite me to speak at your next event. I'm happy to speak at corporate meetings, business associations or societies, and CLE / CPE events.

2. **Get your network documented and audited for free**

   If you're a financial or professional service firm with at least 25 employees or $5 million in revenues, I'll provide a free System Plan and audit of your network. Whether we do other business or not, you get required documentation and a second opinion for your information technology.

Be safe, get educated, and don't be the victim of ransomware!

- Kevin Fream
kfream@matrixforce.com

Made in the USA
Lexington, KY
23 July 2017